DANIEL

FAITHFUL IN THE FIRE

J.D. GREEAR

Lifeway Press®
Brentwood, Tennessee

EDITORIAL TEAM

Reid Patton
Senior Editor & Writer

Brett McIntosh
Associate Editor

Stephanie Cross
Associate Editor

Jon Rodda
Art Director

Tyler Quillet
Managing Editor

Joel Polk
Publisher, Small Group Publishing

Brian Daniel
Director, Adult Ministry Publishing

ISBN 978-1-0877-8361-1 • Item 005842048

Dewey decimal classification: 224.5
Subject heading: BIBLE / PROPHETIC BOOKS OF THE OLD TESTAMENT / DANIEL

Author photo by Andrew Bryant.

To order additional copies of this resource, write to Lifeway Resources Customer Service; 200 Powell Place, Suite 100, Brentwood, TN 27027; fax 615-251-5933; call toll free 800-458-2772; order online at Lifeway.com; or email orderentry@lifeway.com.

Printed in the United States of America

Adult Ministry Publishing • Lifeway Resources • 200 Powell Place • Brentwood, TN 37027

CONTENTS

ABOUT THE AUTHOR

J.D. Greear is the pastor of The Summit Church in Raleigh-Durham, North Carolina. Under Pastor J.D.'s leadership, the Summit has grown from a plateaued church of three hundred to one of over twelve thousand. Pastor J.D. has led the Summit in a bold vision to plant one thousand new churches by the year 2050.

J.D. has authored several books, including *Just Ask* (2021), *What Are You Going to Do with Your Life?* (2020), *Searching for Christmas* (2020), *Above All* (2019), *Not God Enough* (2018), *Gaining by Losing* (2015), *Gospel* (2011), *Stop Asking Jesus into Your Heart* (2013), and *Jesus, Continued...* (2014). He also hosts *Summit Life*, a daily, thirty-minute radio broadcast and weekly NRBTV program.

J.D. completed his PhD in Theology at Southeastern Baptist Theological Seminary. He recently served as the 62nd president of the Southern Baptist Convention. Pastor J.D. and his wife, Veronica, are raising four awesome kids: Kharis, Alethia, Ryah, and Adon.

HOW TO USE THIS STUDY

This Bible study provides a guided process for men and groups of men to discuss the book of Daniel and what we can learn from his story about being faithful in a hostile culture. Eight sessions of study work through the book of Daniel and offer wisdom for men as they seek to embody courage and live faithfully in the places where God has called them as Daniel and his friends did in Babylon.

INTRODUCTORY GROUP SESSION

The first week of study begins with an introductory group session to help establish the group and the course of study. In this introductory session, you'll be introduced to the themes of Daniel and how they influence our lives and Christian men.

Weeks 2–8 follow the format outlined below.

PERSONAL STUDY

BIBLE STUDY

Three days of personal study are provided prior to the group session each week. These personal studies include a prompt to read a portion of Daniel then offer commentary, devotional thoughts, and questions to discover Scripture's meaning and apply it to our lives. Each day of study can be completed in around fifteen minutes.

WRAP UP

The personal study section ends with a reflective activity designed to help members tie together all they've studied during the week.

GROUP STUDY

START

The group session will begin with a few questions designed to help you introduce the session's topic and encourage everyone to engage with the study.

WATCH

This page is left blank intentionally to create space to take notes during the video teaching.

DISCUSS

This section is the main component of the group session. The questions provided are designed to facilitate group discussion about the week's teaching from Daniel.

DISCIPLESHIP GUIDE

A discipleship guide is provided in the back of this resource to adapt the group study for smaller groups of three or four men.

ABOUT DANIEL

AUTHOR

Daniel, whose name means "God Judges" or "God's Judge," was a sixth-century BC prophet living in exile in Babylon. Daniel recounts key events firsthand that occurred during the Jewish captivity and also shares visions that were given to him by God. He likely wrote this book sometime shortly after the end of the Babylonian captivity. Internal testimony supports this claim. In the text itself, Daniel claimed to have written down visions given by God (see 8:2; 9:2,20; 12:5). Additionally, Jesus attributed the book of Daniel to Daniel himself (see Matthew 24:15; Mark 13:14).

BACKGROUND

The historical setting of the book of Daniel is the Babylonian captivity. The book opens after King Nebuchadnezzar's first siege of Judah (605 BC) when he brought Daniel and his friends to Babylon along with other captives among the Judean nobility. Nebuchadnezzar assaulted Judah again in 597 and brought ten thousand captives back to Babylon. In 586 he once again besieged Jerusalem, this time destroying the city, the holy temple, and exiling the people of Judah to Babylon. Daniel's ministry began in 605 when he arrived at Babylon with the first Jewish captives, extended throughout the Babylonian captivity (which ended in 539), and concluded sometime after the third year of Cyrus the Great, the Medo-Persian king who overthrew Babylonia (see Daniel 1:21; 10:1).

MESSAGE AND PURPOSE

The theme of the book of Daniel is the hope of the people of God living in a dark and hostile culture. The book promotes hope by teaching that at all times "the Most High God is ruler over human kingdoms" (5:21). Daniel's purpose was to exhort Israel to be faithful to the sovereign God of Israel. He accomplished this by recounting examples of godly trust and prophecies of God's ultimate victory.

KEY EMPHASIS

Daniel emphasizes that the Lord has dominion over all the kingdoms of the earth, even in evil days when wicked empires reign. Two key words in the book are "king" (used over 150 times) and "kingdom" (used over 50 times). Above all, Daniel teaches that the God of Israel is the Sovereign of the universe, "for his dominion is an everlasting dominion, and his kingdom is from generation to generation" (4:34). Because of this, followers of Jesus can live with hope and confidence in God in a dark and hostile culture.

STRUCTURE

Daniel is narrative book, recounting historical events for the purpose of present and future instruction. The narrative contains history, prophecy, and apocalyptic visions. Apocalyptic literature refers to revelation by God given through visions and symbols with a message of eschatological (end-time) triumph. Although Daniel contains apocalyptic elements, it is not an apocalyptic book; rather, it is a narrative that includes apocalyptic visions.

Noting that the book of Daniel contains both history (chapters 1–6) and prophecy (chapters 7–12), some divide the book into two sections. A better way to view the book's structure is based on the two languages it uses: 1:1–2:3 (Hebrew); 2:4–7:28 (Aramaic); and 8:1–12:13 (Hebrew). The Hebrew sections pertain primarily to the people of Israel, which is fitting since Hebrew was Israel's national language. Aramaic was the international language of that time. Fittingly, the Aramaic section of Daniel demonstrates God's dominion over all nations.[1]

SESSION 1

Faithful

The book of Daniel is about how to be a faithful witness in a dark and hostile environment. You see, unlike other books in the Bible, this book was not written from inside Israel. In the first few verses of Daniel, we learn that God's people had been taken into exile. Following the reign of King Solomon, Israel was stuck in a downward spiral of unbelief, compromise, and disobedience. God warned Israel that if they continued to walk this path, He would send them into exile. And so, in 605 BC, God kept His promise. King Nebuchadnezzar of Babylon laid siege to Jerusalem and took the best and brightest from Israel back to Babylon where they would serve the king who conquered them.

This is where the book of Daniel begins. And yet the book doesn't take us further down the spiral; rather, it shows us that even in the middle of a sinful culture, godly men can follow God and thrive no matter where He's placed them.

The book of Daniel is a manual for how to thrive in Babylon.

KEY IDEA

We can be faithful in Babylon.

START

Use this section to get the conversation started.

Where is the most difficult place you've had to live out your faith?

What do you think it means to live out your faith at work, in your hobbies, or in your relationships?

The book of Daniel is the story of a young Hebrew man abducted from his country and his home to go and serve the wicked king who conquered his people. The book of Daniel doesn't give us a play-by-play of the Babylonian invasion, but we know from history and from other places in the Bible that the Babylonians were ruthless and vicious warriors. They didn't just come in and take over; they used all the instruments of war to bring Judah into submission— killings, torture, starvation. Imagine being in Daniel's place. It would be difficult to thrive in that setting.

But that's just what Daniel did, and that's what God is calling all of us to do. Daniel helps men answer the question, What does faithfulness to God look like in a secular realm controlled by secular powers at war with the gospel?

WATCH

Use this space to take notes during the video teaching.

DISCUSS

Use this section to guide the group discussion.

READ DANIEL 1:1-7.

While Babylon was a city in modern-day Iraq, the Bible also talks about Babylon as a spiritual reality that we all inhabit (see Revelation 18:2,10,21). When have you felt like the culture you live in is a kind of Babylon?

When Daniel and his friends were taken to Babylon, their names were changed to reflect Babylonian culture and heritage. How does the culture we live in seek to conform you to its ways? What are some ways this particularly affects men?

It appears that these young men accepted their Babylonian names without conflict. (Joseph does this as well in Genesis 41:45). How does that challenge our assumptions of what faithfulness looks like in a sinful culture?

How do we determine which part of our culture to accept and which parts to reject?[2]

READ DANIEL 12:3.

Why is ordinary faithfulness to God attractive and noticeable in a dark culture? Can you think of any examples of someone who has shined in Babylon?

What challenges do you face being a faithful witness in the places God has called you?

What does it look like practically to focus on the promise from this verse when it seems like the world is forcing us to make a choice between faithfulness and compromise?

What remaining questions or comments do you have about this session's teaching video? What was challenging, convicting, encouraging, or timely for your current circumstances?

Close your time in prayer.
Remember to complete the personal study prior to the next meeting.

SESSION 2

Different

We've met the central characters in Daniel, and we learned that with God's help we can serve God faithfully in Babylon and that ordinary faithfulness can have a profound impact.

In this session, we'll continue through Daniel chapter 1 and see that we have to be different to make a difference. Our culture will constantly demand conformity to its desires and ways—at every turn it will try to press us into a mold. But men of Christian character are called to break the mold, to stand out. It's the only way we can create change.

KEY IDEA

We have to be different to make a difference.

———————————

DIFFERENT VALUES

Read Daniel 1:1-8.

In 605 BC, God had handed Judah over to King Nebuchadnezzar, who besieged Jerusalem and took Daniel, his friends, and other Jewish nobility back to Babylon in exile. This would have been traumatic and painful for these young Jewish men. Only teenagers, they found themselves in a foreign land with foreign gods and an idolatrous culture.

Yet even though the culture compromised, Daniel and his friends did not. Daniel saw what Babylon valued and determined to live by a different set of values. We read:

> *Daniel determined that he would not defile himself with*
> *the king's food or with the wine he drank.*

DANIEL 1:8

Why would Daniel reject the food from the king's table?

What are some ways cultural values conflict with your faith?

Daniel did not eat from the king's table because the food did not meet the standards God set in His law. In other words, the food was unclean. Because of Christ, we are not held to the same dietary standards (see Mark 7:19). But that doesn't mean our culture won't expect us to compromise. Babylon will always ask us to comprise in the big three—money, sex, and power. Let's consider all three.

MONEY. Babylon approaches money from the standpoint of acquisition: Get all you can; keep all you can; maybe give away a little to show you are a good person and maintain favor with the community. But money is lifeblood, the key to the good life.

Because God is our trust and our treasure, believers have a different attitude toward money. Yes, we live off of money, but we also recognize that money is entrusted to us for the advancement of God's kingdom. So, as God prospers us, we're not just thinking about how to advance our standard of living; we ask how we can advance our standard of giving.

How should Christian men value money differently than our culture?

SEX. Babylon approaches sex from the standpoint of, *It's all about me. If it feels good, it can't be wrong.* The Christian sees sex as a gift of God to be used for God's purposes, according to His design: within a covenant-based, lifelong marriage between a man and a woman.

Early Christians stood in stark contrast to other Roman citizens, because they were "promiscuous" (generous) with their money and guarded with their beds, while other Romans were guarded (stingy) with their money and promiscuous with their beds.

What are some ways men can give in to our culture's attitudes toward sex even if we're not promiscuous ourselves?

POWER. For Babylon, press whatever power you have to your advantage. If it's your looks, use them. If it's your money, use that. If it's your talent, your majority culture status, your minority status, use it. Whatever power you have is to be held onto and pressed for advantage. But the Christian man sees any position of power and privilege like Jesus did—something meant to serve and lift up others.

List some examples of Jesus using His power to serve and benefit others.

PRAYER

God, please help me to be a man who aligns my value with Your eternal kingdom rather than the temporary kingdom of this world.

———————————————————

PERSONAL STUDY 2
INTEGRITY

Read Daniel 1:9-16.

The second way Christian men show we're different is by refusing to compromise our integrity. The four Hebrew men in this passage were likely teenagers, yet they were guided by the strength of their convictions, even when setting them aside would've been "easier" and refusing to do so threatened to cost them greatly.

When they made the request to the king's chief eunuch, he could've had them killed. After all, he was afraid of the king (v. 10) and disregarding or dismissing Daniel's request would've been easier and safer than trying to accommodate it. But Daniel met the man's concern with Christlike compassion. Christians should always hold our convictions with compassion, treating those with different convictions with the same kindness God has extended to us.

Why should we resist the urge to be adversarial toward people who have different convictions than we do?

How might kindness open a door for the gospel?

Holding his convictions gave Daniel favor with the official, but that won't always be the case. This passage is not a promise of a magic formula but an example that points forward to Jesus, who sought peace even with those who reviled Him. He is the One we emulate, and He is the One we pursue. For the follower of Jesus, convictions can't be set aside, because everything we do is done first and foremost as an offering to Jesus, even when it costs us.

Maybe you've heard the story of Eric Liddell, whose story was featured in the movie *Chariots of Fire* (maybe you can hear the theme music now). Eric was an incredible runner who was also a committed Christian, and he was recruited for the 1924 Olympic team for Great Britain. But he soon learned that the hundred-meter qualifying heat was to be held on Sunday, and he wouldn't run on Sunday. His convictions were that Sunday was the Lord's Day and that it would dishonor God for him to run on Sunday. The British team appealed to the Olympic Committee to change the date of the heat, but the Olympic Committee wouldn't budge. It became a big scandal and the British papers skewered him. He became a worldwide laughing stock. His team switched him to the four hundred-meter race, but it was a totally different race that required completely different training. Against all odds, he won. After he won, he said, "Those who honor God, He will honor."

Again, this is not a promise or magic formula. Sometimes you do the right thing and suffer. God often uses our refusal to compromise to show off His power and glorify His name.

In what areas of life would it be easier to compromise your integrity than to hold Christian convictions?

Why should we refuse to set our convictions to the side even if we know other Christians who do?

Can you think of any other examples of men who held their convictions despite cultural pressure? What can you learn from them?

PRAYER

God, may we be men who root our integrity in You no matter the costs.

SCRIPTURE OVER CULTURE

Read Daniel 1:17-21.

What blessing did God bestow on Daniel for following His ways instead of Babylon's?

The third way Christian men show they are different is by conforming to Scripture, not culture. We've seen how Daniel and his friends were removed from Israel and taken to Babylon, where they were expected to conform to its pagan culture. Unclean foods, magicians and sorcerers, and false gods were an essential part of Babylonian culture. Yet Daniel and his friends conformed themselves to the countercultural message of God's Word. Here we have much to learn from Daniel, because the way of Jesus is countercultural in every society.

What are some ways the truth of Scripture is countercultural in our time?

The Bible is an equal opportunity offender—if it hasn't offended you yet, you're not paying attention. In some cultures, it's Scripture's teaching on sexuality that offends the culture. In others, it's the emphasis on grace and generosity and giving away power. In some cultures, it's Jesus's emphasis on the equality of all peoples as made alike in the image of God that offends because this belief threatens to overturn the system. In other cultures, it's God's authority over His creation that offends. No matter the time or the place, we must conform our hearts to Scripture.

When have you needed to adjust your perspective as a result of the Scriptures? Why is shifting our perspective particularly difficult for men?

Our culture will expect different things from us than Daniel's expected of him, but it will press us to conform nonetheless. The question is what we will do with those things our culture requires us to conform to—the "royal foods" it requires us to eat. This is the battlefield where our faith will be tested.

Where is the battle the hottest for you? Where is being different most likely to cost you?

Where are you tempted to shrink back from being different for fear of the cost?

In today's passage following God did not cost Daniel, but as we keep going, you'll see that it will cost him. If we continue following Jesus it will cost us as well (see 2 Timothy 3:12). The way of the cross is different than the way of Babylon.

Why does the cost of following Jesus extend beyond political disagreement? How do we often confuse the two?

Our natural tendency is to think the way of Babylon is the way of the people who disagree with us politically. Resist the urge to think these are just right or left issues. Being shaped by Scripture will put us out of fashion with both parties—neither fully captures the essence of the kingdom of God because both are political parties in Babylon.

There are many things associated with both American political parties that we must profoundly reject. The Christian man doesn't belong to the donkey. The Christian man doesn't belong to the elephant. The Christian man belongs to the Lamb.

PRAYER

*Lord Jesus, help us to be men shaped by Your Word
more than we are shaped by our culture.*

WRAP UP

To wrap up our personal study, here are a few questions to help you consider what it looks like to be different as Jesus was different.

Summarize your biggest takeaway from Daniel 1.

This week we've looked at what it means to be different. To summarize, to be different doesn't mean we need to look like Daniel and his friends. To be different we need to look beyond them to Jesus, the One they point us to. His ministry was a paradox because there has never been anyone who so exalted God's purity and perfection—He said that sooner would heaven and earth pass away than one jot or tittle of God's moral code be compromised (see Matthew 5:18; Luke 16:17)—and yet He effectively gathered the outcast and the nonreligious to Himself. Sinners, prostitutes, and tax collectors flocked to Jesus because He was different. Sinners, prostitutes, and tax collectors flocked to Jesus. He was distinct from His culture.

Christian men are to be distinct from Babylon in relation to sex, money, and power. Use this chart to evaluate how your perspective on these issues is shaped by God or Babylon.

BABYLON	KINGDOM OF GOD
Sex	
Money	
Power	

If we are going to be men who live according to heaven's values, there are some practical places this will show up.

CAREER

How is your work life shaped by the gospel and the Great Commission? If it isn't, how could it be?

Why should you approach your career differently from the people around you?

RESOURCES

How are you using your blessings to bless others?

The people of Babylon used their power and money to take them away from suffering, to isolate themselves from it. For the follower of Jesus, it is the opposite. The trajectory of his or her life moves toward suffering. How can you use your resources to alleviate spiritual and material suffering?

How can you structure your budget so that money is a tool to bless, empower, and prosper the kingdom of God rather than build your own kingdom?

RELATIONSHIPS

Daniel leveraged his relationships to make much of God. What would this look like for you?

START

Welcome to group session 2.

Before starting the new content each week, we'll take a few minutes to review the personal study from this week.

What is one key takeaway from this week's personal study?

How were you challenged or encouraged?

Except for the introductory session, each week's video teaching will summarize and review the personal study leading into it. We'll hear from Pastor J.D. as he pulls the teaching together and helps us connect the truth from Daniel to our hearts and lives. This week we're going to be looking at what it means to be different to make difference.

How would you define what it means to be different or distinct in our culture?

What does it mean to be different in order to make a difference? How is that unlike being different for different's sake?

In the Old Testament, God gave His people the law, which showed them what it was like to live in a relationship with Him. Many of these laws concerning food, clothing, and even labor practices might seem strange to a twenty-first-century reader, but all of them have a purpose. God's people were to be distinct from the nations around them—to be a light to the Gentiles—and to show the world what it looks like to live in a relationship with God. They were called to be different to make a difference. Though Jesus has changed the way we relate to God, the call to be different remains. Let's consider this together.

Pray, then discuss the group teaching together.

WATCH

Use this space to take notes during the video teaching.

DISCUSS

Use this section to guide the group discussion.

READ DANIEL 1:8-21.

Verse 8 tells us that Daniel "determined" to not eat the king's food. Why does being different also require being intentional?

What is the "king's food" in our culture? What are the places in our culture that our faith should lead us to stand apart from?

When Daniel stood apart, he also maintained a relationship with the king's officials that was rooted in kindness and compassion. What can we learn from his example?

How does our culture view the big three—money, sex, and power? How should our faith lead us to see the big three differently than Babylon does?

What steps are you taking to regularly develop your integrity so that you will know when you need to stand apart from culture?

How does accountability in groups like this help us develop character?

What has God been teaching you though the Scriptures recently? How is He equipping you to prize His Word over what our culture values?

How does Daniel's example point us to Jesus?

What remaining questions or comments do you have about this session's teaching video? What was challenging, convicting, encouraging, or timely for your current circumstances?

Close your time in prayer.
Remember to complete the personal study prior to the next meeting.
_____

SESSION 3

Transformation

As we shift into chapter 2, Daniel and his friends had not yet completed their three-year training program in the king's court (see Daniel 1:5), but at this point they had Babylonian names, spoke the Babylonian language, and worked in the Babylonian palace. However, they were doing so as faithful servants of God. And as Christian men in a fallen culture, we can learn a lot from this.

When it comes to living in a hostile culture, many Christians choose either assimilation or separation. Assimilation means you gradually look like everyone else. Their values become your values; your lifestyle imitates theirs. Separation is the opposite. You see the world as evil, so the more isolated you are from the world, the more faithful you believe you are.

Most Christians, like the Jews in Daniel's day, think the only options are either assimilation or separation. But there is a third option: transformation. Transformation happens when we see and believe there is a God in heaven, and His kingdom will continue to shine while all earthly kingdoms fade.

KEY TRUTH

There is a God in heaven, and His kingdom will continue to shine while all earthly kingdoms fade.

A GOD IN HEAVEN

Read Daniel 2:1-28.

Chapter 2 opens with King Nebuchadnezzar waking up in cold sweat. He had that dream again! It wasn't just any dream; it was a nightmare. And every time he had it, he became more upset. What's easy to miss because we're separated from the days of Daniel by centuries, culture, and customs is that dreams were thought to predict future events. A king's dream, therefore, would have ramifications for a nation. Babylonian wise men had this little book with an interpretive key that explained what each element in a dream meant. (A cow meant this and a bird meant this, etc.) So he'd tell them his dream, they'd look up the images in their little book, and BOOM: dream interpretation.

The king consulted the wise men but started to suspect their answers were a bunch of malarkey. If these supposed wise men could not give him the answers he sought, he had no use for them and would have them killed. The problem was that Daniel and his friends were among the wise men. But God had prepared these circumstances for His truth to shine.

> **Look back to verses 14-16. How was the tone of Daniel's response different from the other wise men?**

> **How was his approach to handling the problem itself different (see vv. 17-18)?**

> **Does your response to stressful situations more closely resemble Daniel or the other officials? Explain.**

While most of the royal court responded with alarm, Daniel responded with "tact and discretion" (v. 14). He had a settled peace that allowed him to see the circumstance more clearly than more senior officials. But Daniel wasn't just calm—he urged his friends to join him in prayer. God answered and revealed the mystery of Nebuchadnezzar's dream to Daniel. Scripture tells us:

> *No wise man, medium, magician, or diviner is able to make known to the king the mystery he asked about. But there is a God in heaven who reveals mysteries.*

> **DANIEL 2:27-28**

Could we park there for just a minute on the phrase, "But there is a God in heaven"? That's the most important question, right? Is there a God in heaven, and has He said something to us here on earth? Is there a God in heaven, and is His power available to us? Like Nebuchadnezzar, we all get to a point where every human strategy fails. But we have a God in heaven.

How would it change your problems if you stopped and said, "But there is a God in heaven"?

Which problems or situations in your life do you need to turn over to God in prayer? Remember, these might be more than the big, impossible ones.

Who are some men who might come alongside you in prayer like Hananiah, Mishael, and Azariah (v. 17) did for Daniel?

End your time today praying for the situations you listed above. Then reach out to some brothers in the faith to join you.

PRAYER

Praise the God of heaven that He hears and helps you with your problems.

PERSONAL STUDY 2
A TRUE KINGDOM

In the last personal study, we saw that Daniel was given a supernatural interpretation of the king's dream, which saved his and his friend's lives. Today we're going to read the dream itself.

Read Daniel 2:28-45.

The interpretation of Nebuchadnezzar's dream is an important piece of prophecy because it reveals the core substance of our message to Babylon. Below is a chart that outlines the symbolism in the dream. I'm interpreting this the way many scholars do, but the point isn't, "Who exactly are the toes of this statue?" The ambiguity in the Bible is intentional. If God had wanted us to know more specifics, He would have given them to us. The point is what God is saying to all human kingdoms.

PART	MATERIAL	EMPIRE REPRESENTED
Head	Gold	Babylon
Chest and arms	Silver	Medo-Persian
Stomach and thighs	Bronze	Greece
Legs	Iron	Rome
Feet	Iron and Fired Clay	Dispersed Roman Empire
The Stone	Rock	Future messianic kingdom

Nebuchadnezzar's dream showed a series of successive kingdoms being overthrown and taken over by the one behind it. This side of heaven, we can't know for sure beyond the first two what kingdoms this prophecy referred to, but one thing is perfectly clear in the dream—the stone represented the kingdom of God that stands above and beyond all earthly kingdoms.

What does the description of the stone teach us about our message to Babylon?

Why would this have been relevant to Daniel in his situation?

Consider a few things about this stone. First, the stone was made without human hands; it came about with no human agency. Second, rock is the least valuable substance in the dream— yet this rock came with the power of God, and so it shattered into dust the more expensive metals. Jesus was born poor, never owned a home, and never raised an army, yet He came with the death-defying power of God.

Third, the rock started small but eventually grew into a mountain that filled the earth. When Jesus ascended to heaven, you could put all of His followers into one room. He didn't leave an army or a fortress like Nebuchadnezzar or Alexander or Mohammad. Yet that small movement has swelled into one of the largest religious movement in history.

And that leads us to our core message to Babylon—God sent a Rock to earth called Jesus, who will destroy every false kingdom built by man, whether large geopolitical kingdoms or the independent little kingdom of your own life. As we wait in Babylon, we have the hope and confidence that Babylon is not forever, but the kingdom of our God is.

How will this prophecy help you shine in Babylon?

PRAYER

Thank You, God, for Your everlasting kingdom. May we be men that seek for Your kingdom to come and Your will to be done.

PERSONAL STUDY 3
A VALIDATED MESSAGE

In today's personal study, we'll look at the results of Daniel's interpretation and what that teaches us about how God works in Babylon. The events of Daniel chapter 2 give us another important principle for showing God's work in Babylon: *God validates His message supernaturally in Babylon. Supernatural confirmation is how God distinguishes His kingdom from all the fake ones.*

Read Daniel 2:46-49.

What did Daniel's prophecy teach Nebuchadnezzar about God?

How did Daniel's ability to interpret the dream validate God's work through him?

A wicked pagan king is the last person you'd expect to see worshiping God, but that's how this chapter ends. We'll see in the next chapter that this worship was short-lived, but it's impressive nonetheless. Daniel's determination to remain calm, seek the Lord, and his desire to share the Lord's work with Nebuchadnezzar resulted in the king's worship and Daniel's flourishing in Babylon. Our message today is the same as Daniel's—"But there is a God in heaven" (2:28). As we live in Babylon, relying on the Lord, He will use supernatural means to call people to Himself and validate His message.

How have you seen God validate His message, either in your life or someone else's?

How does Daniel chapter 2 point us to Jesus?

Once again, Daniel's faith, Nebuchadnezzar's dream, and the whole book point us to Jesus. God raised Jesus from the dead to validate His message. If you are in an argument with somebody and one of you dies and rises from the dead, He wins. Like Nebuchadnezzar, you choose whether you'll build your life on that Rock or be crushed by it. There is a God in heaven, and He will destroy every false kingdom made by man. That is true on the societal level and on the personal level.

Now, the irony is, that's not why Jesus came. He did not come to judge us but to die on a cross to save us—to be a rock of salvation we could build our lives on. The rock that the builders rejected became the chief cornerstone for those who put their hope of salvation in Him (see Acts 4:11). The choice is yours—a life of meaning and purpose built upon a rock or a temporary kingdom that will be crushed into powder and washed away with the tide.

Read Matthew 7:25-27.

What parallels do you notice between Nebuchadnezzar's dream and this teaching from Jesus?

What does it look like to build your life on the Rock?

Who do you need to share the message of the Rock with this week?

PRAYER

*Jesus, thank You for being the unchanging Rock I can build
my life on. Please use my life to validate Your message.*

WRAP UP

To wrap up our personal study, here are a few questions to help you consider what it looks like to be different as Jesus was different.

Summarize your biggest takeaway from Daniel 2.

Personal and cultural transformation only happens when you realize that above and beyond your finite problems and struggles, what Daniel told Nebuchadnezzar is also true for you:

But there is a God in heaven who reveals mysteries.

DANIEL 2:28a

Don't let the word *mysteries* trip you up. You're likely not wracking your brain to find the meaning behind a dream, but I'm sure you're in at least one situation in life where you just don't know what to do or where to turn. If not right now, you soon will be.

To end this week of personal study, consider the following prayer prompts and use them to call out to the God of heaven for help in Babylon.

You've tried to make the relationship work. You've tried to fix what is broken. And it's all failed and you feel like there is no hope. Friend, I've got good news, there is a God in heaven.

You've tried to make the kid turn out right. You've told him everything you know to, and you've tried everything you know to make him choose what's right. There's nothing left you know to do. Yes, but there's a God in heaven.

You've tried to overcome that addiction. You've tried to find that missing piece. And you've failed so many times you've started to think, "There is no point!" But—and that's a huge "but"—there's a God in heaven.

Death and disease seem so total, so final. And this year they've taken things from you that you feel like you can never get back. What's the point? Won't death just take us all in the end anyway? Yes, but there's a God in heaven.

You're disappointed in politics. Dismayed by our leaders. Democrats disappoint. Republicans disappoint. Newsflash: if you were put in power, you'd disappoint us too. Yes, but there's a God in heaven.

And speaking of disappointments, let's talk about you. For some of you, no one has disappointed you more than you. No one has lied to you, let you down, or broken promises to you more than you. And you have no confidence to go forward and create a better future than today. Yes, but there's a God in heaven.

Maybe it's a person you know who is far from God, pursuing his sin and himself. You see no way he'll turn to Jesus fully to save him. You tried to tell him the truth, but it has fallen on deaf ears. But there is a God in heaven.

START

Welcome to group session 3.

Before starting the new content each week, we'll take a few minutes to review the personal study from this week.

What is one key takeaway from this week's personal study?

Over the past week, we've read through Daniel 2 and thought about how God can use us as agents of transformation as we engage Babylon. As we work through the group content, consider this question:

If you're at an event where you don't know anyone or are trying something new, are you the kind of person who will jump right in, or does that situation make you uncomfortable and withdrawn?

Everyone has had the experience of being a newcomer at some point, and in those moments, our personalities—whether we're introverted, extroverted, or somewhere in between—determine how we respond. A similar approach plays out as Christians engage the culture God has placed them in. We either move toward assimilating and becoming a part of the culture or separate ourselves entirely from it. However, those aren't the only options. God has given us the grace to be agents of transformation in a hostile culture.

Pray, then discuss the group teaching together.

WATCH

Use this space to take notes during the video teaching.

DISCUSS

Use this section to guide the group discussion.

This chapter in fairly long. Begin by reviewing what takes place in Daniel 2:1-49.

Of the two approaches to culture—assimilation and separation—which do you tend toward? What are the dangers of both?

Daniel followed God in the middle of a hostile culture. What can we learn from Daniel about the path between both extremes? Why is this a needed approach from men in particular?

In verse 10, the king's advisors realized they had no ability to interpret his dream. How do these events—when people reach their limits—present an opportunity for us to share about our limitless God?

What does it look like to share God's wisdom with "tact" and "discretion" (v. 14)?

READ DANIEL 2:28.

Why is the simple truth "But there is a God in heaven" so transformative?

What was the central message behind Nebuchnezzar's dream? What did that mean to him in sixth century BC? What relevance does it have for us today?

Where do you have influence? Where is God leading you to be a transforming presence in your culture? How might God use your faithfulness to validate His message?

What situation do you need to step back and realize, "But there is a God in heaven"?

What remaining questions or comments do you have about this session's teaching video or personal study content? What was challenging, convicting, encouraging, or timely for your current circumstances?

Close your time in prayer.
Remember to complete the personal study prior to the next meeting.

———————————————

SESSION 4

Courage

Great things in the world are only accomplished through courage. Lots of people have great intentions, but those intentions only become reality through courage. How many of you think of yourselves as naturally courageous people? That's not me. I'm usually the "Veronica, did you hear that noise downstairs? You should go check it out" guy. Or, even better yet, I act like I'm still asleep to see if she'll go do it on her own. For most of us, courage is something we have to learn, to develop.

Courage = Confession + Conviction

KEY IDEA

Courage believes not only that God is bigger than the opposition but also better than all alternatives.

CONVICTIONAL COURAGE

Read Daniel 3:1-12.

In chapter 3, we see Nebuchadnezzar hadn't learned much. God revealed (in a dream about a giant statue, no less) to Nebuchadnezzar that his kingdom was fleeting and temporary compared to God's kingdom that will last forever and crush all competitors. After that, the king had a giant gold statue built in his honor and commanded "people of every nation and language" (v. 4) to bow down and worship him. This was all going pretty well for him until three Hebrew teenagers had the courage to reject the king's commands. The central conviction of Christian courage is *Jesus is Lord.*

What convictions led Shadrach, Meshach, and Abednego to reject the king's orders?

How do your convictions shape where to take a stand?

It wasn't the men's faith in God that caused the problem; it was their refusal to *also* acknowledge the divine authority of Nebuchadnezzar. Nothing has changed today: In our Babylon, faith in Jesus is not the problem. It's our insistence that He's the only way of salvation and only source of authority. You will never get in trouble for saying Jesus is your personal Savior. But you will when you say that there is "no other name under heaven given to people by which we must be saved" (Acts 4:12) and that He alone sets the rules about what is right and wrong about sex, marriage, morality, and money.

List some of the idols our Babylon expects men to bow down to and worship.

Why does the supremacy of Jesus threaten these cultural idols?

Every culture and society has its own idols, and the moment you fail to bow down in homage, the fiery furnace awaits. It's the same old spirit of Nebuchadnezzar every time.

In the Smithsonian Museum in Washington, DC, there's a Bible that belonged to Thomas Jefferson with large passages cut out of it. In Jefferson's day, the academic world had turned against any kind of belief in miracles. That was considered unfashionable, uneducated. These Enlightenment thinkers thought the morality of Jesus was awesome—the Sermon on the Mount was the greatest moral treatise in human history. But the miracles were a leftover relic of a superstitious past. If people did this today, they would probably cut out Jesus's teachings on the sanctity of sex and marriage. They'd keep the miracle stories and cut out large parts of the Sermon on the Mount.

Babylon says it is fine to worship Jesus, just edit Him to fit our preferences so you can still bow where you need to bow. But hear me: for the follower of Jesus, that's not an option. He's either Lord or He is not. For us to not make that clear is not just cowardly, it is cruel.

Why is it cruel to be quiet or complacent about Jesus's lordship?

Why do Christian men bear a particular responsibility to stand on the courage of their convictions about Jesus?

These young men understood the call of Jesus and the courage it requires. Because these guys stood when everyone else bowed—even though they got thrown into a fiery furnace for it—an entire empire saw the reality of the God of Israel on display. Scholars say you can trace the faith of the wise men who came to see Jesus at His birth back to this encounter. What will future generations say about the courage and the testimony of our generation? Their eternal future depends on our courage in the present.

PRAYER

Jesus, give me the courage to bow down to nothing but You.

COURAGE DEFINED PART 1

Read Daniel 3:13-18.

Having seen the central conviction of Christian courage—Jesus is Lord—we can go on to define Christian courage. Daniel 3 helps us develop a definition: *Christian courage believes God can and expects that He will but trusts Him if He doesn't.* We'll look at the first two parts today and finish tomorrow. This is defined in verses 17-18:

> *"If the God we serve exists, then he can rescue us from the furnace of blazing fire, and he can rescue us from the power of you, the king. But even if he does not rescue us, we want you as king to know that we will not serve your gods or worship the gold statue you set up."*
>
> **DANIEL 3:17-18**

What must these teenage boys have believed about God to stand against Nebuchadnezzar's decree?

How is what you believe about God intrinsically linked to your courage?

CHRISTIAN COURAGE BELIEVES GOD CAN. Shadrach, Meshach, and Abednego had no doubt who the biggest daddy in this drama was. Their defiance was rooted in their belief that there is only one God and that He is able to deliver His people from any situation. Nebuchadnezzar's threats were nothing compared to the power of their God.

That's the most basic principle of faith: God is bigger than your problems. Any of them. He's bigger than cancer, a lost job, or a broken marriage. He's bigger than sin, shame, and the grave. Not even a hair from your head falls apart from His knowledge or permission (see Matthew 10:29-31).

Where do you need to believe God can?

CHRISTIAN COURAGE EXPECTS THAT HE WILL. These men had no direct promise about what would happen, no huddle where God pulled them aside and told them how it would go down. But they had this suspicion in their hearts that God would deliver them because they understood God's goodness and His willingness to showcase the glory of His name. We have every right to expect that God will act on our behalf. The Scriptures lead us to believe so.

What is the difference between a hopeful expectation that God will act and an overconfidence that God will act in the way you desire?

Can I tell you a little secret? Many of the great feats of faith in the Bible were not done in response to a direct command of God or with a promised guarantee of how things would turn out. Think about how many of Jesus's miracles came about because someone, without a promise or without a plan, took a dare on Jesus's goodness. Think of the woman with the blood disease who came up behind Jesus, believing that if she could just touch the hem of His garment, she'd be healed. She reached out audaciously, taking a dare on His goodness. And Jesus praised her faith and healed her. We don't have to wait for heaven to be rewarded for our faith—we can expect God to break into our lives right now with the evidences of His goodness.

Bold faith doesn't just believe He can; bold faith expects that He will. That's not to say God, in His goodness, never tells us no or to wait. But here in this story, as we see multiple times throughout the Bible, God rewards those who take a chance on His goodness, who "expect that He will."

Where is your faith timid that it could be bold? How does courageous and bold faith lead others to take their own steps of faith?

PRAYER

Father, help me to eagerly hope for Your best,
expecting You will act on my behalf.

_____

PERSONAL STUDY 3

COURAGE DEFINED
PART 2

Read Daniel 3:18-30.

To review, *Christian courage believes God can and expects that He will but trusts Him if He doesn't.* We'll consider the last part of this definition today. Let's look at verses 17-18 again.

> *"If the God we serve exists, then he can rescue us from the furnace of blazing fire, and he can rescue us from the power of you, the king. But even if he does not rescue us, we want you as king to know that we will not serve your gods or worship the gold statue you set up."*

DANIEL 3:17-18

Verse 18 contains the most powerful words in this story and some of the most powerful in the Bible. These teenagers believed God was not only big enough to protect them from Nebuchadnezzar, but they also believed knowing Him was better than anything they'd ever give up. Courage believes not only that God is bigger than the opposition but that He is also better than all alternatives.

Practically speaking, what does it mean for Jesus to be bigger than the opposition?

What about better than all alternatives?

How do these truths form a firm foundation for our courage?

CHRISTIAN COURAGE TRUSTS GOD IF HE DOESN'T. Sometimes you take a stand and God delivers, and sometimes you take a stand and He lets you suffer. The question you have to ask is, *If He lets me go into the fire, is He enough for me?* You see, the only way you'll have the courage to suffer for what is right is if you believe knowing Jesus is enough. This story proves that He is. Though three men were thrown in the fire, there was a fourth man in the flames.

> He exclaimed, "Look! I see four men, not tied, walking around in the
> fire unharmed; and the fourth looks like a son of the gods."
>
> **DANIEL 3:25**

Who was the fourth man, and how did He provide for their security?

How does this encounter point us to Jesus?

There was a fourth man in the fire, and because of Him, the teenagers came out of the flames totally unharmed. Though it says the man looked like a son of the gods, we can say in light of the New Testament that it was the Son of Day. This whole scene prefigures Jesus enduring the cross—Jesus was thrown into the fires of judgment with us. And because He was, we came through judgment totally unharmed.

"Therefore, there is now no condemnation for those in Christ Jesus" (Romans 8:1). The hair on our heads is not singed with judgment; our clothes are not burned. He took the flame so we could emerge in safety, without a trace of judgment anywhere on our bodies or even our clothes. Only the ropes of our bondage to sin burned away! The God who died for you in the fire is the God who will sustain you in the fire.

Is there a fire you're trying to get out of that God intends for you to remain in for the time being? If so, how can you depend on Him to strengthen your resolve?

PRAYER

*God, help me see Your continued goodness to me,
Your ability to protect, and Your ability to preserve.*

WRAP UP

To wrap up our personal study, let's reflect on where the chapter ends.

Nebuchadnezzar exclaimed, "Praise to the God of Shadrach, Meshach, and Abednego! He sent his angel, and rescued his servants who trusted in him. They violated the king's command and risked their lives rather than serve or worship any god except their own God. Therefore I issue a decree that anyone of any people, nation, or language who says anything offensive against the God of Shadrach, Meshach, and Abednego will be torn limb from limb and his house made a garbage dump. For there is no other god who is able to deliver like this." Then the king rewarded Shadrach, Meshach, and Abednego in the province of Babylon.

DANIEL 3:28-30

What resulted from the young men's courage?

A friend of mine says: "Don't search for a faith that will keep you from the fire but for a God that will keep you in the fire." The presence of Jesus was with three Hebrew teenagers in their furnace, and His presence will be with you in any furnace He puts you in also. Again, the God who died for you in the fire is the God who can sustain you in the fire.

The story ends with Nebuchadnezzar commanding all peoples, nations, and languages to gather in unified worship of God's power to save. It's a picture of the future.

After this I looked, and there was a vast multitude from every nation, tribe, people, and language, which no one could number, standing before the throne and before the Lamb. They were clothed in white robes with palm branches in their hands. And they cried out in a loud voice:

Salvation belongs to our God,
who is seated on the throne,
and to the Lamb!

REVELATION 7:9-10

The world will not be unified by the greatness of some earthly kingdom—Babylon, Great Britain, America, or otherwise—but by a Savior who went into the flame of judgment for His people and kept them one hundred percent safe from all harm.

And we help move the world to that worship by determining to bow only to Jesus as Lord, getting up every day believing He can, expecting that He will, and trusting Him if He doesn't. So, my question for you: Where do you need to take a chance on God?

Consider the following situations and reflect on where God might be leading you to take courage and expect Him to work:

reaching out to share your faith at work or at school even though it's awkward

taking a courageous stand at work even though it looks like it will cost you big in the short run

standing for what is right even though it will cost you

persevering in a prayer request . . . believing God's goodness will break in

submitting the application to foster a child even though you're scared about how it'll change your life

boldly choosing to keep pressing on in the marriage even though it's difficult

calling that estranged family member even though you aren't sure how he or she will respond to your offer of forgiveness

confessing your pornography habit to a trusted friend even though you'd rather keep it concealed

making a financial gift God has put in your heart that scares you to death

Where is God leading you to take courage?

START

Welcome to group session 4.

Before starting the new content each week, we'll take a few minutes to review the personal study from this week.

What is one key takeaway from this week's personal study?

Over the past week, we read through Daniel 3 and thought about what it looks like to have God-given courage. As we work through the group content, consider these questions:

How would you define *courage*?

How is courage different than determination? Why must our belief in Jesus be the center of our courage?

Courage is something (we think) we all understand, but is there anything different about Christian courage? If our faith is to shape every aspect of our lives, what does it look like for our faith to shape our courage? As we have seen and will see, true courage is a distinctly Christian belief that is centered in the exclusivity of Jesus and is defined as believing God can and expecting that He will but trusting Him if He doesn't.

Pray, then discuss the group teaching together.

WATCH

Use this space to take notes during the video teaching.

DISCUSS

Use this section to guide the group discussion.

READ DANIEL 3:1-18.

Have you ever found yourself in a situation that—even if it wasn't life-threatening—required courage that would cost you something? If so, share about that experience.

Discuss the relationship between conviction and courage. Why are these two ideas always linked?

What are the gold statues that Babylon expects us to bow to today?

Why is the singularity and supremacy of Jesus the ultimate confession of our courage?

Review the definition of *courage*: Christian courage believes God can and expects that He will but trusts Him if He doesn't.

How was each part of this definition illustrated in this passage of Scripture?

Of the three parts of this definition, which is the hardest for you to believe and trust?

How has God worked in the past to show you He is trustworthy? How do we tune our hearts to draw courage from God that results in trust and courageous obedience?

As you've worked through this chapter, where do you feel like God is calling you to take a dare on Him? How can we support you in that?

What remaining questions or comments do you have about this session's teaching video or personal study content? What was challenging, convicting, encouraging, or timely for your current circumstances?

Close your time in prayer.
Remember to complete the personal study prior to the next meeting.

SESSION 5

Knockout

The first chapters of Daniel follow a familiar structure:

1. Nebuchadnezzar does something that is offensive to God.
2. Daniel or his friends speak into the situation.
3. Nebuchadnezzar comes to his senses and praises God.
4. Nebuchadnezzar returns to his sin.

This week we'll read about Nebuchadnezzar wandering around like a wild beast for seven years, all because of sin God graciously warned him against. God used Nebuchadnezzar to give us a picture of what happens to humanity when we rebel against Him. You see, like Nebuchadnezzar, we were created to rule on earth. But when we reject God and give ourselves to sin, we become like beasts.

So this is not just about Nebuchadnezzar, this is about the whole human race; it's about you and me. This week we're going to reflect on the particular sin that had taken hold in Nebuchadnezzar's heart because it's a problem for us also—pride. We will look at pride's roots, pride's fruits, and pride's cure.

KEY IDEA

Pride in ourselves will keep us from faithfulness to God.

———————

PRIDE'S ROOTS

This chapter (which, incredibly, was written by Nebuchadnezzar) tells of the work God did in the king's life as he wrestled with pride. In His kindness, God issued a warning to Nebuchadnezzar through a dream, but the king did not listen. He was given over to the cost of his sin but was also graciously restored to his right mind and recognized the power of God.

Read Daniel 4:1-33 and list examples of pride you see in this chapter.

Through this passage, we see that pride has two roots. **The first is a failure to see that every good thing comes from God.** Notice what Nebuchadnezzar said:

"Is this not Babylon the Great that I have built to be a royal residence by my vast power and for my majestic glory?"

DANIEL 4:30

Nebuchadnezzar fell for the myth of the self-made man. Why is this a myth?

Why is this a particularly dangerous trap for men?

Many men look out at what we have and say, "I worked for everything I have. Look at what I created by my vast power and for my majestic glory." Yes, we are called to work hard and perform our duties with excellence, but even the slightest moment of self-reflection will show us that the idea of a "self-made man" is not entirely true.

You had no control over the biggest factors contributing to your success—like where or when you were born, the education you received, the society you were born into, the influences that inspired you to succeed, even the genes that gave rise to your talents were gifts from your parents. None of us are truly self-made men. We took gifts God gave us and used them—and to not acknowledge that is plagiarism. Your whole life should have one big footnote: "This came from God, not my doing."

What does it look like to acknowledge that your blessings come from God?

Pride's first root is a failure to see that everything we have is a gift of God. It's always accompanied by a second root—**the foolish assumption that the good life will last forever.**

Nebuchadnezzar assumed he was safe, and relatively speaking, he was. Nebuchadnezzar was the most powerful man in the world in his time. If anyone should have felt secure about the future, it was Nebuchadnezzar. He couldn't be attacked; literally no army in the world compared to Babylon's. He couldn't be fired; he was an unchallenged monarch. He couldn't go bankrupt; he was the world's bank. But you and I both know, God has a way of crushing our prideful assumptions.

What are some assumptions we make about our future?

Nebuchadnezzar faced an unexpected illness. Maybe you've dealt with a similar diagnosis. Our material future is not as certain as we'd like to think. The financial markets can get disrupted. Relationships end. People die unexpectedly. This isn't to say we should go around expecting the worst. Rather, the point is: we're not as invincible as we think. With one small flick of the Almighty's finger, everything changes and your empire will crumble. And in those moments, nothing else matters but God. Those struggles have a way of refocusing our attention.

How has a struggle refocused your attention?

PRAYER

*God, please help me to subdue my pride by acknowledging
that every good and perfect gift comes from You.*

PRIDE'S FRUIT

Read Daniel 4:27-33.

From Daniel 4 and the rest of the Bible, we can identify at least six fruits of pride. It's important to recognize the fruit of pride because fruit can always be traced back to a root.

As you read these fruits of pride, thoughtfully and prayerfully consider which of these show up in your life.

Next, after each one write a potential Spirit-guided response to this kind of pride.

1. COMPETITIVENESS. Nebuchadnezzar's language was filled with boasting: "I, I, my, my. Nobody compares to me." That's the surest sign you are eaten up with pride. I don't mean a healthy desire to do your best but a drive to show you *are* the best. The irony about all this is that you may not even recognize it, but it's obvious to everyone else around you.

Response:

2. INGRATITUDE. The apostle Paul in Romans 1 said that the reason for the fall was that we "did not glorify him as God or show gratitude" (Romans 1:21). Gratitude is a sign of humility. You recognize that everything you have is a gift, and as a sinner you deserve none of it, so you're constantly giving God glory and thanking Him.

Response:

3. ENTITLEMENT. When your life is going well, pride says: "This is as it should be. I deserve this blessing in life. I'm owed this kind of marriage; I'm owed these kinds of kids; I deserve these friends, this job, and so forth. Thank me." And when things go poorly, pride says: "This isn't fair. This isn't right." You live with resentment, blaming others for how they have let you down—your wife, your friends, your kids. You blame God. Pride leads to entitlement; humility leads to gratitude.

Response:

4. OVERCONFIDENCE. Nebuchadnezzar believed his kingdom would last forever. James tells us a sign of pride is that you take the future for granted (see 4:13). A can-do attitude is great, but you can only do anything as God supplies the strength. Paul said it this way: "I am able to do all things *through Him* who strengthens me" (Philippians 4:13, emphasis added).

Response:

5. SELF-WILL. Nebuchadnezzar wasn't afraid to go into the future without God because he believed he had all he needed to make life work, but God showed him how foolish that was. Those who go through life without seeking God's will are those foolish enough to think they can make it in life without him. What's it going to take to wake you up from that insanity?

Response:

6. STINGINESS AND EXPLOITATION. In Daniel 4:27 Daniel pleaded with Nebuchadnezzar to separate himself from his sin by seeking justice and showing mercy. It's significant that Daniel put repentance in terms of a new attitude toward the poor because a sure sign of pride is a callousness toward the needs of others. If you feel like you are responsible for everything in your life, and you have no one to thank but yourself, then you will have no compassion for those who are poor. But if you realize how much you owe to God, your heart will naturally go out to others in need.

Response :

Which fruit of pride do you most often struggle with?

How can you press into the antidote you identified to bring this pride to the Lord?

PRAYER

*Holy Spirit, give me the ability to recognize these fruits
of pride in my life, repent, and seek forgiveness.*

PRIDE'S CURE

Failure and suffering alone were not enough to cure Nebuchadnezzar. Without the right perspective, failure often leads to more bitterness and resentment. God's Spirit has to awaken you in your failure. John Calvin said, "Nebuchadnezzar's insanity alone didn't wake him up. God's Spirit had to give him eyes to see."[3]

Read Nebuchadnezzar's words, paying particular attention to the statements he made about God. Consider circling or underlining them as you read.

But at the end of those days, I, Nebuchadnezzar, looked up to heaven, and my sanity returned to me. Then I praised the Most High and honored and glorified him who lives forever:

For his dominion is an everlasting dominion,
and his kingdom is from generation to generation.
All the inhabitants of the earth are counted as nothing,
and he does what he wants with the army of heaven
and the inhabitants of the earth.
There is no one who can block his hand
or say to him, "What have you done?"

At that time my sanity returned to me, and my majesty and splendor returned to me for the glory of my kingdom. My advisers and my nobles sought me out, I was reestablished over my kingdom, and even more greatness came to me. Now I, Nebuchadnezzar, praise, exalt, and glorify the King of the heavens, because all his works are true and his ways are just. He is able to humble those who walk in pride.

DANIEL 4:34-37

Nebuchadnezzar's final statement is one of the most stunning declarations of humility anywhere in the Bible and worth examining closely.

Notice how it begins: he praised the God of heaven who "lives forever" (v. 34). The king's flatterers had always greeted him with, "O king! Live forever." But now he realized that description only belonged to God. We are only temporary. Our lives are like vapors in the wind, our kingdoms like sandcastles on a beach. God is the only king with "everlasting dominion" (v 34). Trying to erect a life independent of Him is a fool's errand.

How does comparing our finite nature to God's infinite nature bring about humility?

"All the inhabitants of the earth are counted as nothing" (v. 35). God's not impressed with Babylon or America. He has no need of any of us, and our greatest achievements are of no consequence to Him. "He does what he wants with the army of heaven and the inhabitants of the earth" (v. 35). He's fully in charge of history. Armies of angels move at His command, as do the smallest molecules. We're just inhabitants of the earth; God is in control of it.

How do our accomplishments compare to God's? How does the answer to this question lead us into freedom?

"There is no one who can block his hand" (v. 35). God's power is irresistible. Ultimately, no one will ever frustrate His purposes. Not you, not Nebuchadnezzar. Nobody. God does whatever He pleases; no one can stay His hand or say to Him, "What have you done?" (v. 35). God is the only power that can never be thwarted or subdued.

How does seeing God's power allow us to trust Him and let go of pride?

"All his works are true and his ways are just" *and* "He is able to humble those who walk in pride" (v. 37). In the end, the Lord alone will be exalted. The truth of Nebuchadnezzar's story is the mightiest men and women ever to walk the face of the earth will find themselves crumbled in a heap before the King of the Universe, unable even to lift their heads. "so that at the name of Jesus every knee will bow—in heaven and on earth and under the earth—and every tongue will confess that Jesus Christ is Lord, to the glory of God the Father" (Philippians 2:10-11).

That is the conversion testimony of the richest, most powerful, most wicked king in ancient history, but it's our story too. All of us turn from God to pride, but He is able to humble all who walk in pride including you and me.

PRAYER

God, thank You for humbling me. Continue to attack my pride by Your Spirit, yet please build me back up with Christlike humility.

WRAP UP

*To wrap up our personal study, let's reflect on what
Nebuchadnezzar's story can teach us about Jesus.*

And that leads us to the best part of this story. Jesus is the true King. Even though Jesus walked His whole life in submission and humility, at the end of His earthly life God drove Him into the wilderness of suffering, and He died like a beast on the cross. But through His suffering, He brought us life. He forgives our sins and restores our sanity.

When we come to Jesus, not only are we rescued from our sin and self-sufficiency, but also we are given the gift of Christ's humility through His Spirit.

Read Philippians 2:3-11.

> *Do nothing out of selfish ambition or conceit, but in humility consider
> others as more important than yourselves. Everyone should look not
> to his own interests, but rather to the interests of others.*
>
> *Adopt the same attitude as that of Christ Jesus,
> who, existing in the form of God,
> did not consider equality with God
> as something to be exploited.
> Instead he emptied himself
> by assuming the form of a servant,
> taking on the likeness of humanity.
> And when he had come as a man,
> he humbled himself by becoming obedient
> to the point of death—
> even to death on a cross.
> For this reason God highly exalted him
> and gave him the name
> that is above every name,
> so that at the name of Jesus
> every knee will bow—
> in heaven and on earth
> and under the earth—
> and every tongue will confess
> that Jesus Christ is Lord,
> to the glory of God the Father.*
>
> **PHILIPPIANS 2:3-11**

Compare the way Jesus is described in these verses to the way Nebuchadnezzar described God in Daniel 4:34-37. What similarities do you see?

List all the examples of Christ's humility in this passage.

If you are a Christian, the call to "adopt the same attitude as that of Christ Jesus" (Philippians 2:5) is a command. Do you treat cultivating humility as a command? Why or why not?

How are these verses both a protection against and a balm for our sinful pride?

What has Jesus taught you about humility?

Men, as you read this, if you're struggling with pride or have been humiliated through suffering, know the pain you are experiencing is not God trying to punish you for your sin or an indication that He hates you. He's trying to wake you up! He's not trying to pay you back but bring you back! He wants to restore you. If that's you, will you listen?

End today praying through these verses in Philippians.

START

Welcome to group session 5.

Before starting the new content each week, we'll take a few minutes to review the personal study from this week.

What is one key takeaway from this week's personal study?

Over the past week, we've read through Daniel 4 and considered the problem of pride and the grace of humility. As we work through the group content, consider these questions:

What is an accomplishment you're proud of?

What is the difference between a healthy sense of accomplishment and sinful pride?

Men are created and called to subdue the earth (see Genesis 1:28). A sense of accomplishment and the desire for purpose are gifts from God. But like everything else in life, if these God-given gifts are disconnected from their source, they can easily turn into sinful pride. This week, Nebuchadnezzar will provide a case study for us on pride's root, pride's fruit, and ultimately, pride's cure.

Pray, then discuss the group teaching together.

WATCH

Use this space to take notes during the video teaching.

DISCUSS

Use this section to guide the group discussion.

READ DANIEL 4:1-37.

Discuss the two roots of pride—the failure to believe everything comes from God and the foolish assumption the good life will last forever. Where did these roots show up in Nebuchadnezzar's life?

Which of the two roots do you most identify with? How does this most often show up in your life?

Why are men particularly susceptible to these sins?

Define and discuss the six fruits of pride—competitiveness, ingratitude, entitlement, overconfidence, self-will, and stinginess and exploitation.

Next, share which of the fruits you are most prone to. How can we respond to these fruits in a way that honors God and cultivates humility?

How does failure and suffering grow our humility? In those cases, how does Christ use even the most difficult circumstances for our good and His glory (see Romans 8:28)?

Read Philippians 2:3-11. How does pursing Christ in the manner these verses describe help us cut out our pride at its roots?

It has been said that pride is particularly dangerous because those who struggle with it are often unaware. What role do God's Word and the community of faith play in keeping you from pride (and other sins)?

What remaining questions or comments do you have about this session's teaching video or personal study content? What was challenging, convicting, encouraging, or timely for your current circumstances?

Close your time in prayer.
Remember to complete the personal study prior to the next meeting.

———————————————

SESSION 6

Verdict

INTRO TO WEEK 6

The year was 539 BC. Nearly seventy years had passed since Daniel and his friends were brought in chains to Babylon. Daniel was an old man, well over eighty. Nebuchadnezzar was dead—he had been for about twenty-three years—and Belshazzar, his spoiled grandson, was on the throne. Belshazzar was hosting a party—an all-out rager in our terms. Suddenly, a floating hand appeared and etched three mysterious words into the plaster, then disappeared.

As Daniel was brought in to interpret the words, we learn that the message God supernaturally delivered to a wicked king is actually a message from God to people in all times and places.

KEY IDEA

*God has given us a Word from above that gives
right perspective on the present and future.*

PARTYING IN THE FACE OF DEATH

Read Daniel 5:1-7.

The events of these verses are pretty straightforward, if a little weird: King Belshazzar was having a lavish party using the vessels from the temple in Jerusalem as serving ware when a disembodied hand appeared and wrote a cryptic message on the wall. What was happening in the background is less obvious.

Belshazzar *knew* the combined armies of the Medes and the Persians were less than fifty miles away. *Everybody* in Babylon knew that, and everybody was on edge. This was a humongous and well-organized army. So why, in the face of this danger, was Belshazzar throwing a party? We don't know. Maybe he was trying to put on a brave face, to inspire everyone by his courage. Maybe he was trying to drown his own fears in amusement and alcohol. Maybe he was so arrogant that he thought Babylon could never fall.

Why was it so offensive for Belshazzar to use the vessels from Israel's temple?

How does pride play into the self-deception we see from Belshazzar in this passage?

Maybe you remember all the wacky ways people responded to the turning of the millennium at the end of 1999. There was a genuine fear that a Y2K computer bug would cause a global computer crash that would bring civilization to a screeching halt. Some people responded by stockpiling while others responded by partying.

Well, Belshazzar chose the latter and "partied like it was 539 BC" because it's easier to distract ourselves with amusement than face what's going on around us. The issue is that our problems don't go away simply because we aren't thinking about them. The face of death lingers after the party is over.

List some amusements you use to distract yourself from unpleasant thoughts.

Why is it difficult for many men to deal with unpleasant thoughts head on?

In his book *The Denial of Death,* the Jewish atheist philosopher Ernest Becker says that in the face of our own mortality, we usually turn to one of three things to console ourselves. We see all three here with Belshazzar.

First, he said we boast about our **accomplishments** as if those accomplishments give us some kind of immortality. We try to tell ourselves that we've done something that has added meaning to human history, and therefore, will last forever. Belshazzar brought out all the gold and silver they'd acquired from other kingdoms to show that Babylon was special.

Second, Becker said we turn to **romance**. We find meaning in the thrills of sex or the feeling of being treasured by someone. That person's love justifies us, gives us a reason to live. Belshazzar's party was filled with wives and concubines and sex.

Finally, he said we turn to **religion** to show that we're worthy of whatever we will face. We use religion to console ourselves that we're the best of all people and that for whatever comes next, we'll be counted worthy. You can see that in Belshazzar's extravagant toasting of their gods.[4]

Where do you see these distractions in our modern-day Babylon?

Why should Christian men handle unpleasant thoughts differently than Babylon?

The only difference between Belshazzar and us is that he was told the day he would die. We may not know the exact day like he did, but we are just as certain of that day's inevitability. We have one life to live, and how we live matters. Those who know Jesus can live undistracted lives because the end has been written for us.

PRAYER

*Jesus, help me live with the end in mind and embrace
difficulty with a clear mind and an undistracted heart.*

———————————————————

THE SIN BEHIND THE WRITING

Read Daniel 5:9-24.

In a familiar series of events, the wise men were lost, and the queen remembered a man who served Nebuchadnezzar who could interpret this writing. But before Daniel interpreted the message, he explained the nature of Belshazzar's sin that led to the writing on the wall.

Look through verses 17-24. With what did Daniel charge Belshazzar?

Daniel charged Belshazzar with two things that are the essence of all sin:

You have not worshiped God as God. You have not given Him glory and credited Him with all your power and success. You haven't lived your life in response to Him. He has not held first place in your heart. Instead, you worshiped idols because you thought you could control them, and you've lived to please yourself.

You have used what God set apart for His purposes for you own. Specifically, Belshazzar was using knives, plates, and candlesticks for his drunken orgy that had been consecrated to the worship of God.

When have you pursued the same things Daniel called out in Belshazzar's life?

In calling out Belshazzar's sin, Daniel gives us a glimpse into the nature of all sin. This is the writing on the wall for all of us. Yet, God graciously calls us to turn from this sin and toward Him for His wisdom and grace.

For us, these sins are particularly clear in a few areas. Let's consider them.

YOUR TALENTS. You were given gifts and talents to glorify God and serve Him. To not use them for His purposes is like stealing the consecrated things and using them for yourself. All followers of Jesus are supposed to lay down their talents before God and say, "What do You want to do with these?" To not do that is stealing from your Master. God's requirement is a blank check.

What talents has God given you? Where are you using (or where could you use) them to serve Him?

YOUR RESOURCES. "Will a man rob God?" (Malachi 3:8). You were to give back at least the first 10 percent of all God gave you. When don't, God considers it stealing (misappropriation), just like Belshazzar did with the temple vessels. You're misusing a consecrated thing.

Do you give at least 10 percent of your income back to the Lord? If not, why not?

SEXUAL SIN. The body is a sacred thing; it is made in the image of God. For the believer, the body is the temple of the Lord. So, sex is sacred; something you go into with someone after you have fused your whole life with hers in a lifelong covenant. When you use someone else for sexual pleasure, you use a precious thing for your gratification. Belshazzar's story gives you warning of how seriously God takes this.

Read 1 Corinthians 10:31. How should this reshape the way we live every aspect of our lives?

Take a few minutes to consider these areas and confess to God where you need His forgiveness and His Spirit's help to honor Him.

PRAYER

Father, teach me to reject sin and pursue Your wisdom.

GOD'S MESSAGE TO US

Read Daniel 5:25-30.

Now, we need to turn our attention to the writing itself. God preserved the story in the Bible because it's not just for Belshazzar, it's for us too. There's some divine imagery at work here that we need to pick up on. This wasn't the first time "the finger of God" had appeared in Scripture.

In Exodus, when Pharaoh's magicians couldn't duplicate the work God was doing through Moses, they acknowledged the work was from "the finger of God" (Exodus 8:19). Later in the same book, the Ten Commandments were etched in stone "by the finger of God" (31:18). "The finger of God" indicates a power only God has or a direct communication from God Himself.

Fast forward to the New Testament, and we see Jesus doing miracles no one else had ever done—He healed the blind, walked on water, raised the dead, raised Himself from the dead, and He said these miracles proved "the finger of God" was at work among them (Luke 11:20). He claimed that to hear His voice was to hear the voice of God directly.

In Jesus, the finger of God has appeared to this generation. He appeared to us. Jesus's identity was verified through prophecy, miracles, and His resurrection. All of these things show that God is speaking. So what does *Mene, Mene, Tekel,* and *Parsin* mean? Let's take a closer look.

Mene: Your days are numbered.

What do we miss if we don't account for the brevity of our lives? What changes in our lives when we keep a right eternal perspective?

Belshazzar got a rare gift—he was told the day he was going to die. You may not know the day, but your death is just as certain as his. Knowing our time is limited helps us to see all the time we have as a gift to love God and serve others.

Tekel: You have been measured and found deficient.

Read Romans 3:23 and 6:23. Why is knowing our standing before God actually freeing for us?

We can never be righteous enough to tip the scales of God's justice in our favor. But Jesus was, and He willingly took our place on the scale. His sacrifice as our substitute was weighed and found sufficient. Trusting Him with your life and righteousness frees you from working to balance the scales and provides rest for your soul (see Matthew 11:28).

Peres: Your kingdom will end.

Like Belshazzar, everything we're working for will end, but that shouldn't lead us to distract ourselves with amusement; it should lead us to seek the coming kingdom Daniel told us about that will never end. Any investment we make in that kingdom will be returned to us a hundredfold.

How would you summarize the importance of this writing for followers of Jesus?

It's easy to get discouraged in Babylon because everywhere you look, Babylonians are in charge. There were Israelites, like Daniel, who'd lived their whole lives under captivity. And many were wondering, "Is God still in charge? Does He remember us?" You might be asking the same thing. This chapter answers a resounding yes to that question. The days of wickedness are numbered. The true King soon will return, restore justice, and take us home soon to the promised land to spend eternity with Him. Our hope is in that day and that King. Keeping eternal perspective gives us strength to not only survive as exiles, but also to shine as exiles in our dark and hostile Babylon.

PRAYER

*Father, thank You for giving us a Word from You and
a hope that will never disappoint (see Romans 5:5).*

WRAP UP

To wrap up our personal study, let's think about the wisdom
of Babylon and the wisdom from above.

Review Daniel 5:8-24.

The failure of Babylon's wise men to deliver when the questions really matter is a repeated theme in the book of Daniel. Obviously, the wise men contributed something to Babylonian knowledge, or the king wouldn't have kept them around. But when it really mattered, they let the king down. Each of those times, Daniel appeared and revealed that there is a God in heaven who can do what the wise men couldn't. And yet, while we know that in our heads, our lives demonstrate that we value other wisdom more. So let's consider this theme in Daniel to wrap up our week.

How was Daniel described differently than the wise men of his day?

Who would qualify as our wise men?

What are some qualities we look for in our wise men?

How do the qualities you listed above compare to the biblical ideal of wisdom (see Proverbs 1:7)?

There comes a point at which the wise men of every age and every culture fail. Consider two sets of wise men in our Babylon.

SCIENTISTS. To be clear, science and scientists are wonderful gifts of God to be revered and celebrated and trusted in their spheres of authority. But we can also acknowledge that there are places where their authority and expertise fails—or at least it has proven unable to answer questions that we really need answers to. Can science tell you what's right and wrong? Can it tell what your purpose is? No. Only Something that is before the material world and beyond it can give us meaning.

POLITICIANS. Elected officials serve a purpose, but we cannot rely on them to solve humanity's primary problem. Has any political philosophy proved able to correct the human impulse toward corruption, greed, or abuse of power? Our political and educational wise men have proven unable to cure, on any large scale, the problems of the human race at their core, in their source—our hearts.

Just as with Babylon, when it comes to ultimate questions, our wise men—from Stephen Hawking to Steve Jobs to party leaders on the left and right—have failed us. We need a word from God, and we have one: His name is Jesus.

> *Yet to those who are called, both Jews and Greeks, Christ is*
> *the power of God and the wisdom of God.*
>
> **1 CORINTHIANS 1:24**

As we seek ultimate wisdom in Christ, we gain perspective on our lives in light of eternity. C. S. Lewis notes, "If you read history you will find that the Christians who did most for the present world were just those who thought most of the next. . . . It is since Christians have largely ceased to think of the other world that they have become so ineffective in this."[7] If we truly desire to shine in our Babylon, our focus will be on eternity.

By the way, don't forget that the wise men who saw the star in the sky and came to see the baby Jesus were from this region. Babylon had fallen long ago by then, but the traditions and writings of the wise men had remained. Isn't it interesting that somehow in their traditions, they had been taught to look toward heaven for a clue about how the world would ultimately be saved? Encounters like this taught them you have to look toward heaven for ultimate answers. One day, God put a star there, and said, "Here's your answer." And about five hundred years after Daniel 5, a group of them showed up to see the baby Jesus. The encounters in Daniel taught them to look to heaven for the ultimate salvation of the world.

Practically speaking, how do we make it a habit to seek "wisdom from above" (James 3:17) before earthly wisdom?

How will looking to God's wisdom distinguish us from the culture and cause us to shine as Daniel did and as Jesus calls us to?

START

Welcome to group session 6.

Before starting the new content each week, we'll take a few minutes to review the personal study from this week.

What is one key takeaway from this week's personal study?

Over the past week we've read through Daniel 5 and thought about the word God gave a wicked king and the Word God has given us in Christ. Let's consider these questions together as we get started:

When you have big questions or need advice, what is the first place you turn?

How does where we turn or what we do in stress have a way of revealing what's important to us?

Since the garden, we've had a problem of seeking wisdom in the wrong places instead of looking to God and the sources He has provided. God has spoken in previous generations and in our generation. We are responsible for hearing Him.

Pray, then discuss the group teaching together.

WATCH

Use this space to take notes during the video teaching.

DISCUSS

Use this section to guide the group discussion.

READ DANIEL 5:1-30.

Belshazzar and his court partied in the face of death. Why do we have a tendency to distract ourselves with amusement when we're asked to face unpleasant circumstances?

What types of distractions seem to have a particular pull on men in our day? What would you identify as your primary distractions?

What are some ways we can point each other to Jesus when we notice one of us is chasing a distraction instead of dealing with the real problem?

Ernest Becker said that when faced with death we turn to accomplishments, romance, and religion.[6] Give examples of each and discuss why these are ultimately insufficient to help us deal with our biggest problem.

In addition to trying to distract ourselves from our problems, we also have a habit of seeking the wrong wisdom to deal with our problems. What are some sources of wisdom we turn to and why are they ultimately insufficient?

What two sins led to the divine warning Belshazzar received? What do these sins look like in the lives of men today?

Review the writing on the wall in verses 25-28. What was the warning for Belshazzar? What is the warning for us?

How did Jesus provide a more than sufficient answer to the warning in these verses?

What remaining questions or comments do you have about this session's teaching video or personal study content? What was challenging, convicting, encouraging, or timely for your current circumstances?

Close your time in prayer.
Remember to complete the personal study prior to the next meeting.

───────────────────────

Habits

In this session we're going to look at one of the most well-known stories in all of Scripture—Daniel in the lion's den. Babylon had been overthrown by the Medes and the Persians, Nebuchadnezzar and the royal family had all been killed, and King Darius of the Medes now sat on the throne.

Daniel was now well over eighty, still living in captivity in Babylon. We don't know what happened to his friends, Shadrach, Meshach, and Abednego—presumably by this point they'd already died. The new king, Darius, in order to try to bring some continuity and stability to his government, had kept a lot of Nebuchadnezzar's wise men on his court, including Daniel.

As in the past, the king gave an order that Daniel would not comply with because of His faith. From Daniel's response we see that courage is not conjured up in a moment; courage is developed through a lifetime of small, consistent decisions. Courage is a pattern you program into your heart.

KEY IDEA

Courage is a habit of the heart.

COURAGE THAT SUSTAINS

Read Daniel 6:1-10.

List any observations about Daniel's character found in these verses.

Chapter 5 ends with a new king, Darius the Mede, ruling in Babylon. Daniel had continued in public service and continued to field attacks from jealous officials in the king's court. We see this kind of behavior in our election cycles. The commercials start multiplying: "So-and-so is a liar. Thirty-two years ago he said this at a party. He voted with big nursery to take candy from babies." They always seem to find something, but with Daniel, after six decades of public service, these guys searched but couldn't find anything. Daniel had been utterly trustworthy in all that he did.

What did the officials find as Daniel's "weak point"? What must they have known about Daniel to believe this plot would work?

If a decree like this were issued today, in what ways would it challenge you personally?

The weak spot the officials found was Daniel's faith. Daniel had been so consistent after decades in a pagan culture that they had complete assurance that he would be trapped by this law. Their plot appealed to the king's ego and his desire to be seen as a sole provider for his empire. Even though Daniel lived in the king's house, ran his government, and received his meals from the king's table, he never trusted the king as his ultimate provider. For that he looked to heaven, and that's exactly how they trapped him.

Where else in our study of Daniel have we seen him turn to prayer?

What does this teach us about Daniel's spiritual health and habits?

Daniel had prayed three times daily for seventy years. He'd done it in Daniel 1 when they tried to force him to eat forbidden foods. He'd done it in chapter 2 when the king threatened to kill all the wise men because no one could interpret his dream. His friends had done it in Daniel 3 when Nebuchadnezzar tried to force them to bow down to his golden image. Whenever Daniel had been in trouble, he'd turned to God. Prayer was as natural to him as breathing.

What did Daniel believe about God to go to Him in every circumstance, including multiple credible threats to his life?

How does this kind of literal death-defying prayer lead to courage?

Daniel recognized that his life didn't belong to him; it always belonged to God. If that was true, his problems didn't belong to him either; they belonged to God. All Daniel was responsible for and all you're responsible for is what God commands you to do—love and serve Him. When you trust God, the Provider and Sustainer of your life, you can be courageous because you realize everything in life is dependent on Him.

PRAYER

Father, help me to turn to You in prayer, no matter the circumstances.

COURAGE THAT IMPACTS OTHERS

Read Daniel 6:11-24.

In the previous personal study, we saw that Daniel's habit of prayer was not altered by external threats or the might of an empire. Daniel chose prayer because he trusted in God, and that evening he prayed as peacefully as he had every other one. There's a peacefulness in the prayer closet you won't find anywhere else.

When have you experienced peace in prayer, even if your circumstances didn't change?

Compare the peace Daniel had to the energy of the other officials and wise men. What differences do you notice?

Notice throughout this chapter that Daniel was calm while everyone around him was frantic. The other officials knew their trap had worked and couldn't wait to tell the king. Darius saw through their ruse immediately and was "very displeased" (v. 14), but he was also bound by this ridiculous custom. (Note: the law of the Medes and the Persians was actually a safeguard to keep kings from making laws and decrees on a whim. It was irrevocable, not because of stubbornness, but as a means to protect people from unpredictable rulers.)

What evidence is there that Daniel made an impression on Darius?

When the order was made and the judgment was passed, Darius couldn't sleep. You'll notice again that Daniel was at rest while everyone else busied themselves. Daniel took a catnap with all those lions like he was snuggled up in a cadre of kittens. The jealous wise men were up all night partying, the king was up all night worrying, Daniel's friends were up all night praying, the angel was up all night protecting—Daniel was the only one who got a good night's sleep! When the king ordered the stone rolled away from the den the next day, there was Daniel, snuggled up peacefully between the lions.

According to the text, why did God preserve Daniel?

The king was overjoyed when Daniel was saved. Daniel's faith endeared the king to him instead of repelling him. The text tells us that Daniel wasn't delivered because he was special, or because God knew he was writing a Bible story, or because God liked him better than anyone else.

[Daniel] was found to be unharmed, for he trusted in his God.
DANIEL 6:23

You have the ability to trust God as well. You can look for this same kind of providential protection in your life if you pray like Daniel did. That doesn't mean bad things won't happen to you but that God will ultimately deliver you through them all like He did for Daniel. And when God delivers, our trust in Him can make an impact on others.

What are some ways our courageous faith and trust in God makes an impression on others?

Where is God asking you to trust Him? Think of one specific area, write it down, then pray.

PRAYER
Father, I trust You with my life, please sustain me through trouble.

COURAGE THAT POINTS TO JESUS

Read Daniel 6:25-28.

Lists all the truths about God contained in Darius's response to finding Daniel unharmed.

This chapter started with a prohibition on prayer but ends with a pagan king preaching a sermon about God's providential protection. It's actually a pretty good mini sermon. Repeatedly in the book of Daniel, we see amazing sermons preached by formerly pagan kings. And how did they learn these things? They learned them as Daniel and his friends lived with consistency and courage in front of them. Darius declares that God is:

GLOBAL. He's the God of all the peoples, nations, and languages in all the earth (v. 25). Contrary to what the Babylonians believed and twenty-first-century Americans believe, He's not a tribal deity, where "You have your god, and I have mine." This is one God and one truth for all peoples in all times and at all places.

PERSONAL. He's "the living God" (v. 26). He's not like those Babylonian gods that neither speak nor relate to humans—gods that you have to carry around from place to place and leave food in front of. The true God is a living, active, speaking God.

ETERNAL. Not only is He the living God, but He "endures forever" (v. 26).

SOVEREIGN. "His kingdom will never be destroyed" (v. 26).

FAITHFUL. "He rescues and delivers" His people (v. 27).

IMMANENT. "He performs signs and wonders in the heavens and on the earth" (v. 27). This is a God actively at work in the world today, pursuing you and working in your life.

SAVIOR. He "rescued Daniel" (v. 27). This is a God who didn't leave His people to perish in a dark pit but came to them and entered the pit with them. He is ready to help all who call on Him.

And this is what's most important for us. Any time you study an Old Testament character, it's tempting to make the application, "Dare to be a Daniel!" But in Daniel, and everywhere else in the Bible, the point is always Jesus. The Old Testament was not primarily written to give us heroes to emulate but a Savior to adore. When you see the story that way, it takes on new meaning.

List the ways the story of Daniel in the lion's den points us to Jesus.

How would seeking to emulate Daniel actually lead to discouragement, and how does Jesus change what it means to "be like Daniel"?

Daniel and Jesus were both innocent and falsely convicted on bogus charges. Jesus was thrown to the lions of judgment, which circled Him, taunted Him, and then tore Him apart. Unlike with Daniel, no angel came to stand by Him and shut the lions' mouths. Knowing that the Jesus to whom Daniel's life points is with us gives us the courage to face danger like Daniel, to be consistent like Daniel, and to get up and keep going when we've been inconsistent. Jesus, who took your punishment, now promises to preserve you in the den of any lions you face today. With Him, you can have the courage to face anything. Trusting Jesus frees us from sin and striving and gives us Spirit-led courage to shine in Babylon.

PRAYER

God, help me to trust Jesus above all else. Through Your Spirit help me lead a courageous life that points others to Him.

———————————

WRAP UP

To wrap up our personal study, let's consider four possible responses when trouble comes and see some practical ways to implement a God-honoring response.

We will focus more intently on prayer next week, but as we end this week, let's think about Daniel's prayer life and its crucial link to his courage.

*When Daniel learned that the document had been signed, he went into his house. The windows in its upstairs room opened toward Jerusalem, and three times a day he got down on his knees, prayed, and gave thanks to his God, **just as he had done before** [emphasis added].*

DANIEL 6:10

Why is that last phrase so important?

Daniel prayed because it was what he always did. This wasn't as much a response to a terrifying circumstance as it was a daily habit in Daniel's life. It's been said that what you rehearse in times of ease you remember in times of hardship. This is why regular spiritual disciplines like prayer and Bible reading are so important. Habits we cultivate tether us to Jesus and His work in our lives, but these habits need to be cultivated.

To help us cultivate habits of prayer, consider these contrary responses.

PANIC. You get scared and you cave. "Look, there's no way out; the pressure is too strong. All my friends are doing it; I'll be an outcast if I don't. Everybody in my business does it; I'll never survive if I don't." You never need to panic; you're never trapped in a situation with only bad options. God will always provide a way out (see 1 Corinthians 10:13).

PRIDE. This one is tricky because on the outside it can look like bold faith, because you say, "I will not yield to you. I can overcome this." The *difference* between this response and faith is that when you peel back the layers of this response, what you find is not a humble dependence on God but a heart of self-sufficiency. The strongest indicator of pride is prayerlessness.

PREEMPTIVE STRIKE. This is hurting someone before they have a chance to hurt you. Notice Daniel didn't do this, though he likely had the ability to. When Daniel found out about this law, he could have tried to engineer some political trick to get back at them.

If you're honest, what is your instinct when the going gets tough?

How does prayer free us from the other three responses?

Prayer allows us to take our concerns and place them at God's feet so that He can take them up and bear the load for us. So many of us walk around with burdens and lacking courage because we simply will not pray. Like the familiar hymn says:

> *What a friend we have in Jesus. . . .*
> *O what needless pain we bear,*
> *all because we do not carry,*
> *everything to God in prayer!*

However, the good news is that you can begin today. One way to do this is to challenge yourself. Habits are formed through repeated actions. Many of us likely have things we do everyday—exercise, check the news, play a game on our phones, and so on. A habit of prayer can be formed the same way—through practice. Once you start, it will be hard to stop.

Regardless of the status of your prayer life, will you challenge yourself to start a daily prayer time for five minutes a day for the next month? If so, consider the following:

Where will you pray?

When will you pray?

What will you pray about? (Write a few concerns.)

Will you start right now?

START

Welcome to group session 7.

Before starting the new content each week, we'll take a few minutes to review the personal study from this week.

What is one key takeaway from this week's personal study?

Over the past week we've read through Daniel 6 and seen how Daniel prayerfully and courageously defied a government and trusted God in dire circumstances. Daniel was able to do this in part because he had cultivated courage over time through a habit of prayer.

What is a habit you engage in every day?

How have you benefited from that habit?

Most of us are familiar with Daniel in the lion's den. It's among the most well-known and retold stories in all of the Bible. But the entry point into this story is linked to Daniel's refusal to stop praying. When a decree was issued that Daniel could not petition any god or deity other than Darius the Mede, he simply continued praying to God because it was what he had always done. Daniel's courage was developed over a lifetime of prayer. We have the same resources as Daniel to develop courage in our lives.

Pray, then discuss the group teaching together.

WATCH

Use this space to take notes during the video teaching.

DISCUSS

READ DANIEL 6:1-28.

Daniel had formed a habit of prayer that could sustain him through every circumstance. Why is developing healthy spiritual rhythms necessary for growth as followers of Jesus?

Daniel turned to prayer, but we often turn to other strategies when faced with trouble. What are some things we try instead of prayer? Why are they so appealing?

What does it teach us about Daniel's life that his opponents *knew* he would not stop praying?

Reread verse 23. How does trusting God with our lives naturally lead us to trust God with our problems? What problems do you need to entrust to God?

How can we support one another in these hardships? Why does this kind of support sometimes feel awkward or counterintuitive to men?

Repeatedly we've seen Daniel's consistent faithfulness give him personal favor with kings and senior officials. In what ways does genuine faith make our lives attractive and help us shine in Babylon?

What does Darius's statement in verses 25-27 teach us about God? Who is a "Darius" in your life that God might use your faith to reach?

As with every other part of Daniel, the point is not to be like Daniel, but to be like Jesus. How does this chapter in Daniel point us to Jesus? How does linking ourselves to Jesus provide us with courage?

What remaining questions or comments do you have about this session's teaching video or personal study content? What was challenging, convicting, encouraging, or timely for your current circumstances?

Close your time in prayer.
Remember to complete the personal study prior to the next meeting.

SESSION 8

Prayer

Prayer is the most undervalued resource of the church—neglected by many, completely discarded by others. This can especially be true of men. However, Scripture tells us many of the blessings of God are activated in our lives through prayer. It's something we've seen over and over again throughout the book of Daniel. We're going to end our time together by looking at Daniel's prayer in chapter 9.

It's not surprising that at the end of Daniel's book, Daniel circled back around to the power of prayer. It was a running theme of his life, and there's much we can learn from him about this vital spiritual practice. This is a one-of-a-kind passage because it pulls back the curtains and shows us the inner workings of prayer. Yet at the center of prayer is a God who loves us.

The point of this session is to understand that you are greatly loved like Daniel was and to trust God like Daniel trusted Him; then you'll pray naturally and instinctively like he did.

KEY IDEA

Prayer is our first, final, and finest resource.

PRAY GOD'S PROMISES

Read Daniel 9:1-27.

Prayer is the most undervalued resource of the church. Here's a question to think about at the outset of this week of study:

How many blessings for your life or for your family remain unactivated simply because you've never asked for them in prayer?

Whenever I hear older saints—people whose lives you already want to emulate—talking about what they'd do differently in life most say that looking back they wish they'd prayed more. And here we find Daniel at the end of his life praying more. This prayer started because he noticed a promise of God in Jeremiah.

Daniel read in Jeremiah that God would exile His people for seventy years (see Jeremiah 25:11-12). He and his friends were taken into captivity around 605 BC. "The first year of Darius" he referred to in Daniel 9:1 was somewhere around 538 BC, and if you do the math, that means he had been there for around seventy years. So Daniel decided He would pray for what God promised and call on God to take the exiles home. God's promises are there for us today as they were to Daniel. In fact, we have even more because we have the complete Bible.

According to Gabriel, why was God willing to answer Daniel's prayers (see v. 23)?

Incredibly, as Daniel was praying, God sent him an answer directly through the angel, Gabriel:

"At the beginning of your petitions an answer went out,
and I have come to give it, for you are treasured by God."

DANIEL 9:23

Notice how Gabriel started the answer: Daniel, "You are treasured by God." This was the secret to Daniel's consistency in prayer. Sometimes we think our failure to pray is a failure of self-discipline. But at its root, prayerlessness is the result of failing to grasp how much God loves you, how tender He is to you, and how much He wants to hear from you. Prayer is not a way to get close to God as much as it is a response to knowing how close God is to you. That's why Daniel's prayer tied God's glory to His faithfulness to His promises (see vv. 16-17).

What does Daniel teach us about the connection between prayer and Bible reading?

What promises of God are you praying right now?

The Bible is filled with promises, but you have to find them for yourself. I can't do it for you. There are promises about forgiveness and restoration after sin, joy in suffering, godly marriages, parenting, provision in time of need, and many others. Read it for yourself. It's our job to find them and claim them. Effective prayer perceives the gap between where something is and where God wants it to be. Practically this means the quality of your prayer will be directly related to the quality of your knowledge of the Bible. This isn't meant to guilt you into praying or reading the Bible but to show you how connected they are and how God desires to show us Himself though them. Amazing things happen when you take the purposes of God and pray them into reality. The prayers that start in heaven are heard by heaven.

End today spending time in prayer:

Where do you perceive a gap in what God's Word says He wants and where your life is now (in your marriage, in your kids, in your job, etc.)?

Pray for this need saying, "In _____ as it is in heaven."

PRAYER

Father, "Your kingdom come. Your will be done on earth as it is in heaven" (Matthew 6:10).

DON'T GIVE UP

Read Daniel 9:20-27. Pay particular attention to verse 21.

While I was praying, Gabriel, the man I had seen in the first vision, reached me in my extreme weariness, about the time of the evening offering.

DANIEL 9:21

What state did Gabriel find Daniel in? Why does that matter?

List all the times we've seen Daniel pray throughout this study.

When Gabriel arrived, Daniel was exhausted because he'd been praying for seventy years at this point. And Jesus said he was in good company. Throughout the Scriptures, God teaches us that some answers to prayer only come through persistent asking. Jesus compared it to a neighbor who shows up at your house to borrow PopTarts™ from you at 3 a.m. and the only reason you get up and help that person is because you know he is not going to leave you alone (see Luke 11:5-13). Jesus also compared effective praying to a woman who gets a settlement from the judge only because he knows she will to come to his door day and night until he responds to her request (see Luke 18:1-8). Jesus said, "That's how you should pray." Persist in asking.

Does your attitude toward prayer match the persistence of the people in Jesus's parables? Why do we often feel like our requests are tiresome to God?

Persistent prayer is a feature throughout the Bible. In fact, it continues in the book of Daniel.

Read Daniel 10:10-13.

What does this teach us about the way our prayers are answered?

Why is it good that we don't know all the particulars of how prayer works?

Daniel had prayed for twenty-one days with no answer, when he got to entertain another angelic messenger because the first one got caught up in other business. These verses raise a lot of questions, but what we're meant to take from them is that God is always active and listening. It may be that He has sent angels to take care of it, but they are delayed for some reason. Either way, we have good reason to persist in prayer—both because Jesus told us to and because we have biblical examples of God answering on His own timeline.

Have you ever looked back with gladness that God didn't answer a prayer in your time? How did that build your faith and trust in Him?

What request have you made repeatedly to God that you're still seeking answers on? Write them down and then spend a few minutes praying, knowing God loves you and hears you.

The point is, who knows what is happening up there as you pray? So you've prayed for twenty days with no answer. Keep praying. Help is on the way. You've prayed for sixty-nine years with no answer. Keep praying. God gives some things only in response to persistence in asking. You say, "Why does He do it this way?" I don't know. Maybe it's to test our resolve. To see how much we actually trust Him. Or to see how quickly we'll turn away from God and pursue some other means. Don't give up. He promises never to turn you away. Don't give up on year sixty-nine. Who knows what is happening up there.

PRAYER

Lord, I know You are not slow as others count slowness
(2 Peter 3:9) but are always loving and faithful. Please
answer these requests in Your way and in Your time.

———————————

PERSONAL STUDY 3

PRAY IN VIEW OF GOD'S MERCY

Read Daniel 9:17-18.

What Daniel says in verse 18 might be one of the most significant "secrets" of prayer:

*Listen closely, my God, and hear. Open your eyes and see our desolations and
the city that bears your name. For we are not presenting our petitions before you
based on our righteous acts, but based on your abundant compassion.*

DANIEL 9:18

For what reason did Daniel expect God would answer him?

How does that change the way we pray?

God doesn't answer our prayers because of who we are or how we pray but because of who He is. The longer I walk with Jesus, the less confident I grow in my abilities to change people, and the less convinced I am of my worthiness to demand anything from God. When I first started out in ministry, I was pretty confident. I thought, "If I just explain this to them the right way, with the force of my personality, I can change this person." Y'all, I can't even keep myself in the path of righteousness, much less get somebody else. So I pray, "God, I'm not asking You to work in this person's life according to the measure of my abilities. And I'm certainly not asking You to reward me for my righteousness, because I don't really have any. No, give to me according to the abundant riches of Christ's mercy. According to the abundance of His capabilities." Because that's a well that will never run dry.

Why is this attitude freeing for those of us who struggle in prayer?

How does praying "In Jesus's name" connect our prayers to God's mercy?

That phrase "In Jesus's name" is not just a little verbal signal to God that you're about done, like saying, "In conclusion." That's what many Christians think. When you say, "In Jesus's name," You are saying, "God, I'm not praying according to my worthiness but Yours. My hope is not in my righteousness or ability—so I bring this prayer, not in my name, but in Yours. I'm not asking this based on my worthiness to receive it but Your worthiness to give it."

What thoughts about prayer have you discovered through this study that you need to correct?

Friend, **you** are greatly loved, and you are treasured by God. I know that because Jesus came to die on a cross for you to save you out of your sin, if you are willing to receive that. Give up trying to make yourself worthy for God to hear and just receive His grace to you as a gift in Jesus. It's ready for you. Once you do, God is ready for your burdens, and when you pray, the angels move. Reading about it is great, but the most important thing we can do is act on it. And that's how I want to challenge you to end your day.

What request do you need to bring to God? What is burdening your heart? Pause for a moment to still yourself, then approach God with the confidence that you will be received by the God of the universe in the throne room of heaven—all because He loves you and is merciful toward you.

PRAYER

God, thank You for receiving me as a perfect Father
receives a beloved son, in Jesus's name.

———————————————

WRAP UP

To wrap up our personal study, let's consider some things
we've learned walking with Jesus through Daniel.

CONSISTENCY is key.

Daniel's remarkable life all goes back to a couple of rather mundane decisions he made as a young man. First, he resolved not to defile himself in the king's palace with the things God had forbidden. He determined that he would not compromise his convictions to get ahead in the palace. At several points that resolve threatened his future career, but his refusal to compromise was the place where God came through for him.

In what areas of life do you need to remain consistent to shine in Babylon?

What are the things you've determined not to defile yourself with in order to love and serve God?

DISCIPLINE is key.

Daniel prayed daily. Every day, no matter what was going on, he opened his window toward Jerusalem and prayed three times a day. From that daily time with God, Daniel drew an enormous amount of strength. This discipline characterizes all great men and women of God— even Jesus. The Gospels tell us that whenever Jesus needed strength or wisdom, He retreated by Himself to pray. The biggest practical difference between success and failure in your life might be setting your alarm clock thirty minutes earlier so you can read the Bible and pray before starting your day.

How has studying Daniel helped you develop spiritual disciplines or think differently about them?

How do these small practices supply us with the strength to shine in Babylon?

CONSISTENCY and DISCIPLINE are key, but God is the point.

The goal of prayer or consistency or any spiritual discipline is not just to check a box or to give you a chance to dump information on God that He already knows. The point is designating time to be *with* Him. To commune with Him. To have His Spirit fill your mind and heart with His wisdom and strength. Strength from God comes only from time with God.

Ultimately, what drove Daniel to be faithfully committed to God in a place where everyone around Him was not?

Daniel was exiled, forced to serve in the court of a pagan king. Yet he remained faithful to God because he believed none of the circumstances in his life meant God hadn't been faithful to him. Daniel understood that God loved him. He understood that God was merciful, compassionate, faithful, and true to His Word. He was able to shine because of who caused him to shine—not because of anything that was in him but because of what was in the One greater than Him.

What about you—where is God calling you to be faithful? How can you show the Babylon you live in the glory of the God you serve?

START

Welcome to group session 8.

Before starting the new content, we'll take a few minutes to review the personal study from this week.

What is one key takeaway from this week's personal study?

Over the past week we've read through Daniel 9 and seen how courage is a habit cultivated out of other habits. This week we're going to conclude our study by pressing into one such crucial habit that we've seen throughout the book of Daniel: prayer.

Why do you suppose most people, even people who claim no religion, pray?

Do you remember when you first learned to pray? Who taught you?

Does prayer come naturally to you or is it a habit you'd like to develop more consistency in?

Prayer is a vital practice for Christians because it connects our hearts to God's will in a way that nothing else does. It's a practice most people engage in but would hope to do more. Imagine what would happen if Christian men became devoted to the practice of prayer. The goal of this session is not for you to learn how to pray more or to prayer better but to help you see God's heart for you in a way that will draw you to Him.

Pray, then discuss the group teaching together.

WATCH

Use this space to take notes during the video teaching.

DISCUSS

READ DANIEL 9:1-27.

One of the central ideas of this session is that prayer is one of the most undervalued resources in the church. Why do you think that is?

Consider your own life—what is going on in your heart and life when you are prayerless?

Why is it significant that Daniel prayed because he understood he was "treasured by God" (v. 23)? How does that same truth apply to us? How should it transform our prayer lives?

What is the connection between Bible reading and prayer? How do we engage in both out of love for God rather than a sense of guilt or duty?

In this chapter, Daniel was in the twilight years of his life. Why should we persist in praying even when we feel like there's no answer? Who has modeled this well for you?

What does the book of Daniel teach us about persistence in prayer? Share with the group at least one thing you've been praying for over a long period of time. Consider stopping right now to lift up those requests to God.

Read verse 18 again. Why is it essential that we link God's willingness to answer our prayers to His compassion toward us? What do we miss if we make it about something else?

What have you learned about prayer over the course of this study that will help you be more consistent in prayer? How can the other men in this group support you in that?

What remaining questions or comments do you have about this session's teaching video or personal study content? What was challenging, convicting, encouraging, or timely for your current circumstances?

What is one key takeaway you have from this study that you've taken to heart or plan to implement in the days ahead?

Close your time in prayer.

_____

DANIEL

Discipleship
Guide

TIPS FOR LEADING A SMALL GROUP

Follow these guidelines to prepare for each session.

PRAYERFULLY PREPARE

REVIEW. Review the personal studies and group questions ahead of time.

PRAY. Be intentional about praying for each person in the group. Ask the Holy Spirit to work through you and the group discussion as you point to Jesus each week through God's Word.

MINIMIZE DISTRACTIONS

Create a comfortable environment. If group members are uncomfortable, they'll be distracted and therefore not engaged in the group experience. Plan ahead by considering the seating, temperature, lighting, food or drink, surrounding noise, and general cleanliness

At best, thoughtfulness and hospitality show guests and group members they're welcome and valued in whatever environment you choose to gather. At worst, people may never notice your effort, but they're also not distracted. Do everything in your ability to help people focus on what's most important: connecting with God, with the Bible, and with one another.

INCLUDE OTHERS

Your goal is to foster a community in which people are welcome just as they are but encouraged to grow spiritually. Always be aware of opportunities to include any people who visit the group and to invite new people to join your group. An inexpensive way to make first-time guests feel welcome or to invite someone to get involved is to give them their own copies of this Bible study book.

ENCOURAGE DISCUSSION

A good small group experience has the following characteristics:

EVERYONE PARTICIPATES. Encourage everyone to ask questions, share responses, or read aloud.

NO ONE DOMINATES—NOT EVEN THE LEADER. Be sure that your time speaking as a leader takes up less than half of your time together as a group. Politely guide discussion if anyone dominates.

NOBODY IS RUSHED THROUGH QUESTIONS. Don't feel that a moment of silence is a bad thing. People often need time to think about their response or to gain courage to share what God is stirring in their hearts.

INPUT IS AFFIRMED AND FOLLOWED UP. Make sure you point out something true or helpful in a response. Don't just move on. Build community with follow-up questions, asking how other people have experienced similar things or how a truth has shaped their understanding of God and the Scripture you're studying. People are less likely to speak up if they fear that you don't actually want to hear their answers or that you're looking for only a certain answer.

GOD AND HIS WORD ARE CENTRAL. Opinions and experiences can be helpful, but God has given us the truth. Trust God's Word to be the authority and God's Spirit to work in people's lives. You can't change anyone, but God can. Continually point people to the Word and to active steps of faith.

KEEP CONNECTING

Think of ways to connect with group members during the week. When people move beyond being friendly to truly being friends who form a community, they come to each session eager to engage instead of merely attending.

When possible, build deeper friendships by planning or spontaneously inviting group members to join you outside your regularly scheduled group time for activities, meals, group hangouts, or projects around your home, church, or community.

FAITHFUL

KEY SCRIPTURE: Daniel 1:1-7; 12:3

KEY IDEA: We can be faithful in Babylon.

KEY QUESTIONS

While Babylon was a city in modern-day Iraq, the Bible also talks about Babylon as a spiritual reality that we all inhabit (see Revelation 18:2,10,21). When have you felt like the culture you live in is a kind of Babylon?

When Daniel and his friends were taken to Babylon, their names were changed to reflect Babylonian culture and heritage. How does the culture we live in seek to conform you to its ways?

How do we determine which part of our culture to accept and which parts to reject?[7]

What challenges do you face being a faithful witness in the places God has called you?

KEY CHALLENGE

Here at the outset of the study, ask God to help you identify places where you might have the opportunity to shine in the Babylon He has placed you in. What relationships can you forge here? What challenges might you expect? How might God overwhelm and overcome those challenges?

What's something God-sized that you might hope and expect God to do through your ordinary faithfulness?

SESSION 2

DIFFERENT

KEY SCRIPTURE: Daniel 1:8-21

KEY IDEA: We have to be different to make a difference.

KEY QUESTIONS

Verse 8 tells us that Daniel determined to not eat the king's food. Why does being different also require us to be intentional?

What is the "king's food" in our culture? What are the places in our culture that our faith should lead us to stand apart from?

When Daniel stood apart, he also maintained a relationship with the king's officials that was rooted in kindness and compassion. What can we learn from his example?

How does our culture view the big three—money, sex, and power? How should our faith lead us to see the big three differently than Babylon does?

What has God been teaching you though the Scriptures recently? How is He equipping you to prize His Word over what our culture values?

KEY CHALLENGE

How do we know the difference between being different and being weird? In the Bible, we are called to be distinct or set apart. What does that look like in the places where you have influence?

SESSION 3

TRANSFORMATION

KEY SCRIPTURE: Daniel 2

KEY IDEA: There is a God in heaven, and His kingdom will continue to shine while all earthly kingdoms fade.

KEY QUESTIONS

Of the two approaches to culture—assimilation and separation—which do you tend toward? What are the dangers of both?

Daniel followed God in the middle of a hostile culture. What can we learn from Daniel about the path between both extremes?

In verse 10, the king's advisors realized they had no ability to interpret his dream. How do these events—when people reach their limits—present an opportunity for us to share about our limitless God?

What does it look like to share God's wisdom with "tact" and "discretion" (v. 14)?

Read Daniel 2:28. Why is the simple truth "But there is a God in heaven" so transformative?

What was the central message behind Nebuchnezzar's dream? What did that mean to him in sixth century BC? What relevance does it have for us today?

KEY CHALLENGE
Two things:

Where do you need to apply "but their is a God in heaven" to your own life?

What position or influence—however big or small—has God given you? How might you leverage the Spirit's work inside of you to bring renewal and transformation in the places?

SESSION 4

COURAGE

KEY SCRIPTURE: Daniel 3

KEY IDEA: Courage believes not only that God is bigger than the opposition but also better than all alternatives.

KEY QUESTIONS

Have you ever found yourself in a situation that—even if it wasn't life-threatening—required courage that would cost you something? If so, share about that experience.

Discuss the relationship between conviction and courage. Why are these two ideas always linked?

What are the gold statues that Babylon expects us to bow to today?

Review the definition of courage: Christian courage believes God can and expects that He will but trusts Him if He doesn't. How was each part of this definition illustrated in this passage of Scripture? Of the three parts of this definition, which is the hardest for you to believe and trust?

Why have people through time found that they need to take a dare on Jesus's goodness to them? What can we learn from it?

KEY CHALLENGE

As you've worked through this chapter, where do you feel like God is calling you to take a dare on Him? How can we support you in that?

KNOCKOUT

KEY SCRIPTURE: Daniel 4

KEY IDEA: Pride in ourselves will keep us from faithfulness to God.

KEY QUESTIONS

Discuss the two roots of pride—the failure to believe everything comes from God and the foolish assumption the good life will last forever. Where did these roots show up in Nebuchadnezzar's life? Which of the two roots do you most identify with?

How do these most often show up in your life? Why are men particularly susceptible to these sins?

Define and discuss the six fruits of pride—competitiveness, ingratitude, entitlement, over-confidence, self-will, and stinginess and exploitation. Next, share which of the fruits you are most prone to. How can we respond to these fruits in a way that honors God and cultivates humility?

It has been said that pride is particularly dangerous because those who struggle with it are often unaware. What role do God's Word and the community of faith play in keeping you from pride (and other sins)?

Do we feel permission to call each other out on pride? Why or why not? How might this practice build faith?

KEY CHALLENGE

Spend some time this week doing a self-diagnostic on your own pride. Where is there pride in your heart? How can you replace it with something more productive for your own soul and for the kingdom of God?

VERDICT

KEY SCRIPTURE: Daniel 5

KEY IDEA: God has given us a Word from above that gives right perspective on the present and future.

KEY QUESTIONS

Belshazzar and his court partied in the face of death. Why do we have a tendency to distract ourselves with amusement when we're asked to face unpleasant circumstances?

What types of distractions seem to have a particular pull on men in our day? What would you identify as your primary distractions?

How do our distractions keep us from thinking about what is truly important? How might the devil be using these as a strategy to keep men from pursuing God?

What are some ways we can point each other to Jesus when we notice one of us is chasing a distraction instead of dealing with the real problem?

Review the writing on the wall in verses 25-28. What was the warning for Belshazzar? What is the warning for us?

How did Jesus provide a more than sufficient answer to the warning in these verses?

KEY CHALLENGE

Take an account of your own distractions—whether sports, gaming, work, friends, or any number of things. What are they keeping you from? How are you a less effective servant of the Lord because of them? How should the urgency of eternity shape the way we view our distractions?

HABITS

KEY SCRIPTURE: Daniel 6

KEY IDEA: Courage is a habit of the heart.

KEY QUESTIONS

Daniel had formed a habit of prayer that could sustain him through every circumstance. Why is developing healthy spiritual rhythms necessary for growth as followers of Jesus?

Daniel turned to prayer, but we often turn to other strategies when faced with trouble. What are some things we try instead of prayer? Why are they so appealing?

Repeatedly we've seen Daniel's consistent faithfulness give him personal favor with kings and senior officials. In what ways does genuine faith make our lives attractive and help us shine in Babylon?

Who are building relationship and rapport with outside the faith? How can we make genuine friendship with others a spiritual habit without turning those friendships into a project?

As with every other part of Daniel, the point is not to be like Daniel, but to be like Jesus. How does this chapter in Daniel point us to Jesus? How does linking ourselves to Jesus provide us with courage?

KEY CHALLENGE

It has been said what we repeat in times of ease, we remember in times of hardship. What habits are you developing now that will help you when life becomes difficult?

SESSION 8

PRAYER

KEY SCRIPTURE: Daniel 9

KEY IDEA: Prayer is our first, final, and finest resource.

KEY QUESTIONS

One of the central ideas of this session is that prayer has the ability to move heaven and earth. When have you seen prayer be this effective?

Consider your own life—if prayer is truly effective, what is going on in your heart and life when you are prayerless?

Why is it significant that Daniel prayed because he understood he was "treasured by God" (v. 23)? How does that same truth apply to us? How should it transform our prayer life?

What does the book of Daniel teach us about persistence in prayer? Share with the group at least one thing you've been praying for over a long period of time. Consider stopping right now to lift up those requests to God.

Do you set aside regular time with nothing else to do but pray? Do you pray regularly with others or with family? If so, what have you gained from that practice? How has God changed you through it? If not, why not?

What is one key takeaway you have from this study that you've taken to heart or plan to implement in the days ahead?

KEY CHALLENGE

What are you expecting God to do that can only be accomplished through prayer? How can we join one another in that?

END NOTES

1. Adapted from: Michael Rydelnik, "Daniel," in *CSB Study Bible: Notes*, ed. Edwin A. Blum and Trevin Wax (Nashville, TN: Holman Bible Publishers, 2017), 1321-1323.

2. Joyce G. Baldwin, *Daniel: An Introduction and Commentary*, vol. 23, *Tyndale Old Testament Commentaries* (Downers Grove: InterVarsity Press, 1978), 90.

3. John Calvin and Thomas Myers, Commentary on the Book of the Prophet Daniel, vol. 1 (Bellingham, WA: Logos Bible Software, 2010), 295.

4. Ernest Becker, *The Denial of Death* (New York: The Free Press, 1973).

5. C. S. Lewis, *Mere Christianity* (New York: HarperOne, 2015), 135.

6. Becker, *The Denial of Death*

7. Baldwin, *Daniel: An Introduction and Commentary*, 90.

SOURCES CONSULTED IN THE ORIGINAL SERMON SERIES

BOOKS

Mark Batterson, *Circle Maker*

Tim Chester, *1 Samuel For You: For Reading, for Feeding, for Leading*

Sidney Greidanus, *Preaching Christ from Daniel*

Chris Hodges, *The Daniel Dilemma*

Beth Moore, *Daniel: Lives of Integrity, Words of Prophecy* (Bible study)

Larry Osborne, *Thriving in Babylon*

John Sailhammer, *NIV Compact Bible Commentary*

SERMONS

Daniel Akin, "Back to the Future"

Steven Furtick, "Daniel 3"
Steven Furtick, "Daniel 6"

Timothy Keller, "The Prayer for David"
Timothy Keller, "The Dream of the Kingdom"
Timothy Keller, "The King and the Furnace"
Timothy Keller, "Pride: The Case of Nebuchadnezzar"
Timothy Keller, "The Finger on the Wall"

Bryan Loritts, "Standing in Babylon"
Bryan Loritts, "Gone Too Soon"
Bryan Loritts, "Cultivating Babylon"
Bryan Loritts, "Making History in Babylon"

John MacArthur, "The Rise and Fall of the Word, Part 1"
John MacArthur, "Divine Graffiti: The End of an Empire"
John MacArthur, "Daniel in the Lions' Den"

Tim Mackie, "So Righteous—Faithfulness in Exile"

Daniel Simmons, "Faith in the One True God Endures Through All Adversity"

OTHER MEDIA

Tim Mackie, The Bible Project, "Overview: 1 Samuel"
Jen Wilkin, "Introduction" The Village Church Bible study on 1 Samuel

If only Solomon had written a book on wisdom.

Oh, wait.

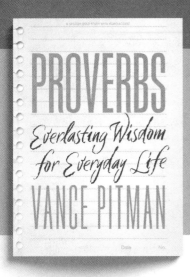

Take a month-long journey through all 31 chapters of Proverbs. You'll not only gain an appreciation for this popular and applicable book of the Bible, you'll also begin to develop a daily habit of seeking wisdom from God's Word. In addition to the four session videos, you get access to 31 short, daily teaching videos (one for each chapter), all included in the purchase price of the *Bible Study Book*.

Learn more online or call 800.458.2772.
lifeway.com/proverbs

Lifeway

Become a beacon in a world of despair.

Christian men should not be separating from the world but transforming it by standing up against the contrary messages the culture puts in front of us.

ADDITIONAL RESOURCES

BIBLE STUDY EBOOK WITH VIDEO ACCESS
005842049 **$19.99**

DVD SET
005845642 **$29.99**

In this study you'll:

- See the role men play in shaping our world for the better.
- Learn to live faithfully in a hostile culture.
- Embrace and trust in the sufficiency of Jesus.
- Develop courage that withstands testing and spiritual adversity.
- Better understand the book of Daniel.

STUDYING ON YOUR OWN?

To enrich your study experience, be sure to access the videos available through a redemption code printed in this *Bible Study Book*.

LEADING A MEN'S GROUP?

Each group member will need a *Daniel Bible Study Book*, which includes video access. Because all participants will have access to the video content, you can choose to watch the videos outside of your group meeting if desired. Or, if you're watching together and someone misses a group meeting, they'll have the flexibility to catch up.

Browse study formats, a free session sample, video clips, church promotional materials, and more at lifeway.com/danielstudy.

Price and availability subject to change without notice.

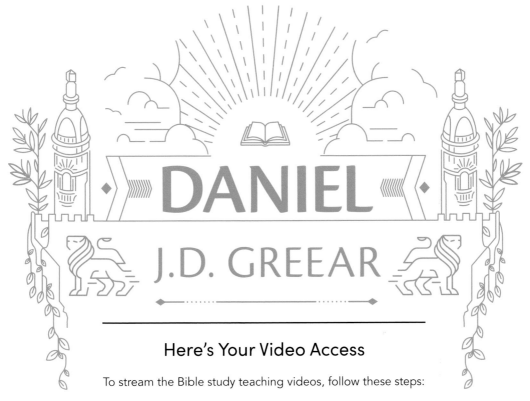

Here's Your Video Access

To stream the Bible study teaching videos, follow these steps:

1. Go to my.lifeway.com/redeem and register or log in to your Lifeway account.

2. Enter this redemption code to gain access to your individual-use video license:

B D F 2 V D L 6 R X

Once you've entered your personal redemption code, you can stream the Bible study teaching videos any time from your Digital Media page on my.lifeway.com or watch them via the Lifeway On Demand app on a compatible TV or mobile device via your Lifeway account.

There's no need to enter your code more than once! To watch your streaming videos, just log in to your Lifeway account at my.lifeway.com or watch using the Lifeway On Demand app.

QUESTIONS? WE HAVE ANSWERS!
Visit support.lifeway.com and search "Video Redemption Code" or "Video Streaming FAQ" or call our Tech Support Team at 866.627.8553.